Black Hol... ... ~.~............~

"A thoughtful, thought provoking look at the perils today's organizations face if they choose to ignore the fundamental actions that help to support their business."
—*Ross Wace* Partner,
Wace & Associates Ltd.

"To achieve continued exponential growth requires the highest performing organizations. *Black Holes in Organizations* provides insights into popular pitfalls to avoid."
—*David G. Thomson*
Author, *Blueprint to a Billion*

"Ron Lutka takes us to the middle of an organizational 'black hole' only to discover that it is inhabited by *people*. Our staff, customers, suppliers, and stakeholders all have the ability to help create the destructive black hole—but they are also the key to getting organizations out of the dark matter we create. Ron provides the clarity owner/managers need to snuff out 'time bombs' and align organizations for success."
—*David S. Simpson, MBA*
Executive Director, The Business Families Centre
The Richard Ivey School of Business, The University of Western Ontario

"We experienced a few black holes within our own organization this year and when we discovered them it was too late, and costly. Too bad that I did not read the book *Black Holes in Organizations* before for it could have avoided me pain and made our company more profitable. Be pro-active, this book is an 'ought to have' if you want to have a streamlined company."
—*Danny Boulanger*
President and CEO, Business Architecture, InterDoc Corporation

"Just when leaders in business and industry thought they thoroughly understood organizations, another major breakthrough is made—a breakthrough in organization functionality and corporate governance."
—*Walter Ramka, FCI, CICP*
Associate Director (Credit & A/R Mgmt), Bell Canada

"Lutka's work on black holes resonates with me, having spent time wrestling with data integrity issues, business controls, operations management, and the decision-making process. All four would be better served by the removal of black holes, as would my anxiety level. Surprisingly, the concept of black holes as presented by

Lutka is easy to understand. More surprisingly, in my experience, pervasive black holes receive little or no attention."

—*Robert Hutton CMA*
Controller, Balmer Architectural Mouldings

"Ron Lutka's *Black Holes in Organizations* provides the reader with insight into the many causes of black holes that impede the success of business organizations. The reader of the book will have the opportunity to apply these causes specifically to his or her organization. Black holes are created by people. With proper support and encouragement, people can implement the remedial action to eliminate black holes. The book provides the reader with many examples as to how to eliminate black holes."

—*Robert W Babensee CA*
Retired Partner, BDO Dunwoody LLP

"Black holes do exist because we find them in many companies while preparing continuity plans. They can mean the difference between recovering the business or going out of business after a disaster. Ron raises the awareness of black holes and the effects they can have on a business. As Ron points out, if these holes continue to exist, then the future of the business cannot be guaranteed under normal or abnormal circumstances."

—*Michael Wilkovesky*
Principal, Business Continuity & Recovery Consulting

"Ron Lutka deftly illuminates the destructive nature of organizational black holes that inevitably arise, and if untreated, fester and linger like a cancer within the belly of the business enterprise. Usually ignored and often never recognized for the damage they can create, these 'black holes', off the radar screen of management, continue to silently undermine the effectiveness of the organization.

"Like a good physician Ron Lutka carefully diagnoses the illness he labels as 'black holes'. He presents comprehensive lists of examples for detecting broken systems and unfixed problem areas and then proceeds to offer us the healing cure. With his Corporate Streamlining Technology we are given a sensible, practical and consistent methodology to remedy organizational black holes at the level of root causes. Any business manager, owner, operational or financial executive truly committed to pursuing excellence and to improving their organization should pay very close attention. No matter the size of your business or its current state, there is much offered here to re-shape and re-vitalize your organization."

—*Brian Gallinger, B.Ed., CGA*
Controller, Brydson Group of Companies

Black Holes
in Organizations

BLACK HOLES
IN ORGANIZATIONS

Define Dissect Diffuse

The internal destruction of organizations,
and its effect on
you!

Ron Lutka

iUniverse, Inc.
New York Lincoln Shanghai

Black Holes in Organizations
Define Dissect Diffuse

iUniverse books may be ordered through booksellers or by contacting:

iUniverse
2021 Pine Lake Road, Suite 100
Lincoln, NE 68512
www.iuniverse.com
1-800-Authors (1-800-288-4677)

ISBN-13: 978-0-595-42536-5 (pbk)
ISBN-13: 978-0-595-86865-0 (ebk)
ISBN-10: 0-595-42536-4 (pbk)
ISBN-10: 0-595-86865-7 (ebk)

Printed in the United States of America

First Edition, 2007

Cartoons by Glick-Art, Toronto, Canada
Alex Glikin, Director, www.bookspluskids.com

This publication is designed to provide accurate and authoritative information with regard to the subject matter covered. It is sold with the understanding that the author and publisher are not engaged in rendering legal, accounting, or other professional advice. If legal advice or other expert assistance is required, the services of a competent professional should be sought.

—Adapted from a "Declaration of Principles" jointly adopted by a Committee of the American Bar Association and a Committee of Publishers and Associations.

To order this book please visit our website at www.blackholebook.com or the publisher's website at www.iuniverse.com/bookstore.

First printing

For passionate executives

"Most organizations that have black holes for some time also have heroes within their ranks that management is likely unaware of. These heroes possess a high degree of responsibility, something opposite to the 'withered responsibility' mentioned above."

—Excerpt from Appendix A, Section xxv, "Crib Notes Are Holding the Organization Together"

CONTENTS

FOREWORD

In over thirty years as a senior officer of a number of companies that varied in size and business scope, I have observed a seemingly endless list of structural problems that hindered corporate performance. You would think that with the authority endowed to the senior executive, it would have been easy to make the necessary changes. Not so! For positive change to occur you need to support it with a sound foundation. All too often that foundation is ignored.

Many books have been written about the optimization of corporate profit. These range from visioning to strategic planning to objectives-setting and more. They provide excellent insights into the opportunities that can be created for an organization. However, they seldom demand that the executive burrow down to the core activities that are the mainstay of the organization—the foundation, which, if made to function effectively, will support and nurture the changes that need to be made. Most often, the responsibility for design and implementation is left to the middle-level staff or consultants with little incentive to strive for a comprehensive and long-lasting solution. The priority for middle management is to achieve quantity as quickly as possible, normally expressed in dollars, but not the quality that sustains the desired results over the long run.

For change to be successful it must be made in a manner that promotes successful behaviour up the entire hierarchy. Success is not measured in only dollar terms. In fact success is more about people feeling good about their efforts and wanting to contribute. Feeling good starts with the knowledge that their roles have a legitimate and positive relationship with the goals of the company. Instead, how many employees today see their roles as less than productive or of dubious value? And, how have these negative feelings been compounded by the downloading of even more dubious work associated with the typical reorganization that stresses quantity at the cost of quality.

Ron Lutka's book speaks about working at the core, about understanding the objectives and building the foundations that will support behaviour consistent with the goals of the company. In so doing, I have witnessed the satisfaction that employees derive from knowing that their efforts have meaning, and, because of this, their attitudes and energy increase the momentum of the organization.

It requires a lot of energy to undertake Ron's mission, but the rewards for the organization can be greater than ever imagined.

Axel Breuer
Vice President, Hino Motors Canada, Limited

PREFACE

This book is not about teaching. It is a book about observing. It is about helping you observe. Perhaps you, too, see a black hole in your organization—perhaps not. You can draw your own conclusions in your own time. You can choose to act or not to act based on your conclusions. You are powerful. You possess the ability to reason, judge, conclude, and act. Who am I, or anyone else, to tell you what to do or how to do it? I will simply state my case concerning the area of organizational functionality based on my experiences among the executive crowd, in the middle-management "trenches", and among the supervisory and worker "weeds". You can take it from there—or leave it.

My research consists predominantly of on-site experience both as an employee and as a contractor (assigned various accounting and financial capacities or hired to improve organizational functionality). This was augmented with feedback received from various sources, including customer employees, retired executives, streamlining students, co-workers, information technology specialists, and business associates confirming the existence of black holes or black hole-like activity.

At some point, the ball started rolling downhill as the data about black holes began to line up. Black holes began revealing themselves in many forms and at odd times: executives were admitting low-level failings were hampering their initiatives; business-improvement projects were continuously over budget and under delivered; clerks were expressing frustrations arising from numerous simple breaks and disconnects; customers grew dissatisfied as products and services deteriorated; more time and employees were required to perform the same tasks; accountants resigned because their numbers could not be supported at the grass roots level and had to be adjusted. Black holes explained a lot.

Contained within these pages are many observations and a handful of conclusions that, if acted upon, just might ease your burden. I will leave that for you to tell me. As a minimum, readers will be given the opportunity to understand what black holes in organizations are—entities with borders and force and character.

—Ron Lutka
author@blackholebook.com
Toronto, Canada
March 2, 2007

ACKNOWLEDGMENT

The author expresses sincere thanks to

Harish Chauhan,
creator of UPh,
founder and president of Business by Philosophy

for his insistence that this book be written
to expose black holes in organizations.

INTRODUCTION

This book has three main purposes:

- To alert senior executives and directors to the *possibility* that a black hole exists in their organization
- To give senior executives, middle managers, supervisors, and frontline workers the *vision* required to determine if a black hole is forming, or has formed, in their organization
- To help organizations *reduce the destruction* that black holes can cause

However, there was another reason for writing this book: to bring some humanity, purpose, and pride into an all-too-often cold and neglected workplace, and to do so in a way that ensures everybody wins. Making widgets may not be a tremendously rewarding human endeavour, but it can be—as can many other endeavours for those who are functioning as part of a well-trained, in-control, highly productive, tightly-knit unit that operates on a basis of fairness and produces wanted and needed products and services.

By shifting attention from the cog side to the human side of the enterprise equation, we can align organizations so that consumers receive what they need—quality products at fair prices—and employees feel productive and infused with pride, dignity, and passion. In short, there are business and personal rewards to be gained by caring—caring about an executive faced with difficult challenges and choices, about proud and passionate entrepreneurs struggling to remain afloat, or about clerks who are frustrated by the demands of placing square pegs in round holes.

The cog has an inherent flaw. It can never be better than it was the day it was produced. It can only deteriorate through wear and tear and neglect. On the other hand, that magnificent life force—the human being—can help an organization prosper. The dynamic human being, not the static cog, is the *only* force that can align an organization with its purpose. If that were not amazing enough, the human being has the ability to diagnose and repair its flaws and those of cogs and other static parts. A cog is never "new and improved" without human innovation. Which deserves more of your attention—the "human being" or the "static cog"?

PART I

In a Nutshell

CHAPTER 1

WHAT ARE BLACK HOLES IN ORGANIZATIONS?

The *Oxford Dictionary of Current English*, third edition, defines a black hole as "a region of space having a gravitational field so intense that no matter or radiation can escape."[1, 2, 3]

Whereas astronomical black holes suck up matter and energy, black holes in organizations suck up valuable resources, including human energy, time, space, materials, and money. A black hole is a significant entity, not something to be ignored. One ignores black holes in an organization at his or her peril and, unfortunately, at the peril of many innocent people.

Definition of a Black Hole

A black hole in an organization can be defined as follows:

> An area of an organization where there is, unbeknownst to management, an abundance of undesirable activities or a lack of desirable activities, both of which destroy organizations.

Three Basic Components

A black hole in an organization includes the following components:

1. *Destruction* in some form occurs within the organization, whether in the form of undesirable activity or a lack of desirable activity.

2. There is an *abundance* of undesirable activity, or a lack of abundance of desirable activity, not merely an occasional occurrence.

3. Management might or might not be aware of the destruction, but management definitely has an *absence* of awareness of the root cause of the destruction.

Hidden Aspect of Black Holes

Management is often not aware of the root cause of a particular form of destruction in the organization. Management might see a lot of busy people but little production and not know why this is occurring. Or management might see inventory increasing despite sales declining but not know why. Management might see the destruction, but if a black hole exists, management will not be able to see the root cause.

Known problems definitely warrant management's attention; however, unknown problems are far more insidious, because management cannot solve or resolve what it does not know or cannot define. This is why black hole destruction festers and compounds and creates great damage to the organization and its people.

Many organizational failures are internal, yet they are erroneously explained away as "cash flow problems", "deteriorating margins", or "increased competition" in a tone that states nothing can be done about it. The fact that it is so difficult to detect a black hole festering away within an organization is one reason why a black hole is so harmful. It is also why management, in trying to solve the result of the problem and not the root cause, does not take effective action or takes incorrect action sometimes. It is easy to understand management's misdirected energy, for the presence of black holes makes it difficult to distinguish the cause of a problem from the result, due in part to the long, interrelated chain reactions involved.

To make matters worse, in reaction to the existence of black holes, some employees, managers, departments, and entire companies erect a façade, intentionally or unintentionally, which shields the black hole. In either case, the underlying reality is far different from the appearance. The appearance is one of "everything is fine," "everything is under control," and "no problems here." There is a sense of calm, even serenity. Yet, the reality can be damage, inaccuracy, impairment, bottlenecks, risk, loss, ignorance, failure, and most likely write-offs.

Concealment Aspect of Black Holes

Black holes disguise and conceal large problems and opportunities. As you read through this book, please keep this concept in mind: *Reducing a black hole in an organization leads to the discovery of or better understanding of larger problems and opportunities.* Once a black hole is diminished, the organization becomes more transparent and often, one finds that there is an earlier source to the larger problems and opportunities. An understanding of the situation leads to and clarifies the later problem. These viewpoints are essential to properly understand and resolve the larger problems and for the organization to capitalize on its opportunities. This theme is repeated throughout the book and is a central focus of our efforts.

Finally, black holes redirect the attention of management and employees. Instead of discovering and acting upon large problems and opportunities, they spend their time coping with mere "end of the wisp" disruptions. Eliminating black holes will free up resources that can then be used to address larger problems and opportunities.

For example, while unearthing black hole-creating items at one company, management discovered that very expensive capital equipment was down regularly, delaying existing orders and threatening the business. Someone had failed to replenish maintenance parts stock items, as required by standard operating procedures (cause). This condition persisted for so long that everyone involved had forgotten these procedures existed. As a result, critical items were being ordered only on an emergency basis—i.e., when the equipment failed (end-of-wisp effect). We took action by replenishing the parts stock which began to reduce excessive machine downtime.

Pervasiveness of Black Holes

Almost any department in an organization—such as pricing, service and installation, shipping, production, storehouse, inspection, marketing, contract administration, data entry, estimating, or purchasing—can have black holes, and they can even create larger black holes that permeate the organization. If a black hole is department-specific, management would be wise to diffuse it quickly before it spreads throughout the organization. If ignored and left to fester, eventually it *will* spread throughout the entire organization, acting as a drag on performance and a drag on reaching the organization's goals.

Repeated undesirable activities not only cause problems, they also disguise opportunities. Within organizations, there can be numerous black hole-creating items, exceeding what this one book can outline. However, if you suspect that your organization is caught in a black hole from which it cannot escape because management is unaware of its existence, then you can use this book to raise awareness about black holes within your organization.

~ Chapter Summary ~

Historically, black holes have been elusive and pervasive. By clearly defining what a black hole is, we can direct our attention to specific aspects of organizations, thereby removing the power that black holes hold. Once a black hole has been lessened, larger problems and opportunities often become exposed, clarified, and easier to repair or capitalize upon.

Armed with a basic knowledge about black holes, management will be able to determine if the organization it has been entrusted to steward is financing a black hole or is being sucked into one.

CHAPTER 2

WHAT CAUSES THE FORMATION OF BLACK HOLES?

There is only one big-picture reason why black holes form in organizations. That reason is "entropy." However, black holes actually form when entropy exceeds "syntropy" in a particular environment.

Syntropy and Entropy

Some forces build organizations up, like an accountant who balances the books or a president who increases sales. Other forces tear it down, like the few employees who do not complete basic work or who pass along inaccurate information, or competitors who steal your ideas.

The human body is a constant battle between syntropy and entropy. A force is working hard to compose the body into an organized and functioning arrangement of cells (syntropy), while the environment is trying to tear down the body (entropy). Sugar and other foods rot teeth. Knees get scraped on earth's terrain. Windblown skin dries and then withers. Blows break bones.

> *Syntropy*
> a tendency toward harmonious association in an open system
>
> *Entropy*
> a tendency toward disorder or randomness in an open system

Disease attacks the body. Dietary-induced cholesterol clogs arteries, and hearts stop pumping.

At any given moment, both forces are at work within an organization. If the syntropy forces do not overwhelm the entropy forces, then over time, the organization can become shapeless and disorganized.

Two distinct classes of entropy can impact the functional health of organizations:

1. Large sudden-impact factors, or *big change events*

2. Smaller but ongoing *subtle factors*

Big-Change Event Entropy

Big-change event entropy is like an earthquake or tsunami hitting and destroying the organization, or at least causing noticeable disruption. For example, in what seems like a positive move, businesses at times launch new and lucrative product lines within a short period, overwhelming the people who must design, cost, produce, package, market, sell, deliver, service, and account for the new products in accordance with the president's promises to customers. Despite their goodness, mergers, acquisitions, expansion of operations, restructuring, computer conversions or implementations, and sudden booms in sales are classic big-change events.

Subtle-Factor Entropy

Subtle-factor entropy is like corrosion eating away at the inner walls of water pipes. You may not know it is there until it compromises a complex manufacturing process. It is like the lime buildup in water pipes that slows, and then eventually jams the water flow. If not addressed, the "water pipes" in an organization can leak, burst, or jam anywhere in the network, even in multiple locations. Suddenly the network of tasks and responsibilities that make up a functioning organization seizes up or bursts, and the organization ceases to function, or functions under great duress.

It would be inaccurate to claim that one of these two classes of entropy—subtle-factors or big-change events—is more destructive or devastating than the other.

Failing to be honest with customers regarding delayed deliveries is an example of subtle-factor entropy.

Internal Forces and External Forces

Most of the syntropy within organizations is internal—management and employee generated. Entropy, however, can be equally internally and externally generated.

Whether the causes are intentional or unintentional, and whether they are socially good or bad, powerful external forces can exert entropy upon an organization that is trying to survive and prosper. These forces include the following:

1. Governments
2. Competition
3. Suppliers
4. Financial institutions
5. Unions
6. Customers

Basic Building Blocks

To understand basic building blocks, one must burrow down to the micro level of organizations. Management conducts research on the economy, market forces, and competition, and then surveys its resources. Next, management plans strategy. Strategy leads to execution. *Below* execution lie the basic building blocks of organizations which enable execution to occur and upon which everything else rests. If one understands these concepts, then one understands this book.

Whether the entropy forces mentioned above are internal or external, a result of subtle factors, or a big-change event, black holes are formed by the same mechanism: *a breakdown of basic, usually repetitive activities of the organization at the "micro" level.* Several micro-level failings can lead to the formation of a black hole. However, failings at the micro level receive very little attention, and so they are allowed to stack up and choke organizations. A disciplined, systematic approach to observation and data collection would unearth such failings. This approach will be discussed further in chapter 4, "Relief from Recurring Problems."

A string of incidents in which damaged goods are shipped to customers can be black hole-creating items, especially if they result in claims filed by customers. Why were the goods damaged? Why were the goods shipped? The action of damaging the goods is a black hole-creating item. It is an undesirable activity. The action of shipping the damaged goods is a black hole-creating item, too, one that is often overlooked. It too is an undesirable activity; however, it might have been preceded by a lack of desirable activity, such as proper inspection.

It is the micro-level breakdowns that often become black hole-creating items. And when enough black hole-creating items are "in play," a black hole has formed in the organization. *A black hole invariably leads to much larger problems*, such as narrowing margins, cash-flow problems, difficulty preparing a meaningful budget, unhappy customers, inefficiencies, bitter employees, large write-offs, and a "clouded" organization (where management questions the reliability of its decision-making source data).

Basic micro-level activities are the building blocks of organizations. When enough of them fail, the organization fails, yet they receive so little attention. In what way can these building blocks fail? Below are common types of basic micro-level failures in organizations:

More actions than necessary

More actions than necessary: A regional manager of a unit spending $30 million per year approves every purchase order, contract, and invoice instead of delegating low-value approvals to a subordinate.

Damage caused: The regional manager is overwhelmed by the paperwork, which causes him to lose control over costs.

Wrong action

Wrong action: Packaging material used to protect a product during shipping and handling is inadequately applied.

Damage caused: Product is damaged, customers return products, and the company experiences lost sales, and lost profits.

Symbiotic actions disconnected

Symbiotic actions disconnected: An inaccurate representation of manufacturing abilities is communicated to sales personnel.

Damage caused: The sales staff make promises to customers that the company could not deliver on.

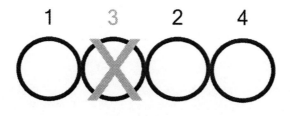

Wrong sequence

Wrong sequence: Orders are priced and accepted prior to collecting cost data.

Damage caused: Some orders are overpriced (resulting in lost sales) and other orders are under priced (resulting in narrow or negative margins).

Unexpected action

Unexpected action: A new brand of enamel being applied to products blisters and peels.

Damage caused: Company suffers lost sales and lawsuits.

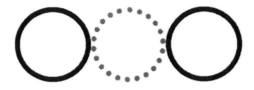

Omitted action

Omitted action: No one was assigned the responsibility for maintaining a computer system.

Damage caused: Over time, numerous bugs crept into the computer system, which frustrated users. The system fed inaccurate data into the enterprise reporting system, which in turn led to poor decision making.

Incomplete action

Incomplete action: A newly hired marketing coordinator received only 40 percent of the training needed for the job.

Damage caused: The marketing coordinator misinformed sales and marketing staff as to how much money was approved for spending in their regions. Subsequently, the organization spent 30 percent more on marketing than it had budgeted for.

The diagram below portrays the connection between micro-level failures and their threat to an organization's survival. This is an extremely simplified diagram. When a significant black hole is present, the *volume* of micro-level failures is usually many times greater than shown in the diagram, and the damage caused not only flows up, as depicted in the diagram, but also flows *down* and *sideways*. The downward- and sideways-flowing damage can occur, for example, when micro-level failures cause the distribution of inaccurate data throughout the organization and, as a result, poor decisions are made exacerbating the organization's problems, including those found at the micro-level.

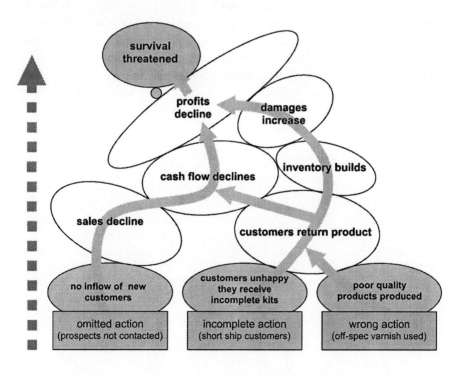

Connection between micro-level failures and their threat to survival.

Aggravating Factors

The many-layered pyramid structure of modern-day organizations contributes greatly to subtle-factor black hole formation. Today's organizational charts place those with the most responsibility (executives) the furthest away from what they are responsible for (the functioning of the organization). It is as if executives are looking through the wrong end of the telescope. At that distance, it is difficult for executives to see what is going on within their sphere of responsibility.

There is another aggravating factor that allows black holes to form: organizational management and assisting professionals have yet to accept an organic view of organizations. Management places heavy attention on the academic accomplishments of their employees and the speed and accuracy of machinery—both necessities. Yet, they place little attention on badly needed organizational functionality and an understanding of organizational dynamics.

~ Chapter Summary ~

Given that entropy causes black holes to form in organizations, the key to resisting the formation of black holes (or to eradicating black holes that exist) is to allow the forces of syntropy to overwhelm the forces of entropy—before the entropy forces overwhelm the organization. Organizations that have never performed a search for black hole-creating items will likely be suffering from the negative effects of an accumulation of breaks in the basic building blocks of organizational functionality. These breaks can be caused by both big-change events and subtle-factor entropy.

CHAPTER 3

DAMAGE CAUSED BY BLACK HOLES

The damage caused by black holes is multi-dimensional, therefore the damage can be explained in many different ways. However, the true damage caused by black holes is usually more serious than we could describe in a few words. Furthermore, this true damage is elusive, as the cause of one problem could be the effect of another root cause. To give the reader a glimpse of the damage black holes can cause, three types of damage will be discussed: mechanical, structural and results damage. Any way we look at it, black holes hold organizations back from reaching their long term goals.

Mechanical Damage

The following is an example of a series of mechanical functions for a typical organization:

1. Receiving goods from a supplier
2. Verifying that all goods were received, and in good order
3. Signing the receiving documents

To be more precise, we could further break down each of the above mechanical functions into additional mechanical functions. For example, Step 1, "Receiving goods from a supplier," can be broken down as follows:

1. Arrange for a receiver to arrive at work to receive goods.

2. Properly train receiver on receiving goods.

3. Provide the receiver with the necessary tools to inspect and receive goods.

4. Ensure trucks can access the receiving area to unload goods.

5. Arrange scheduling of receiving goods so the receiving process does not become bottlenecked.

6. Provide receiver with contact names and numbers in case the receiver is in doubt about an incoming truck.

Some of the above mechanical functions can be further broken down and should be reviewed during a proper search for black hole-creating items. Often, *those* mechanical functions can in turn be broken down. Can the receiver read a bill of lading? Does he know which documents to staple together and where to file them, or to whom he must give them? When addressing black holes, we must deal with them at a very low level, for minor problems in volume are often the root source of larger ones. This topic was mentioned in chapter 2, "What Causes the Formation of Black Holes?" and will be discussed further in chapter 4, "Relief from Recurring Problems."

The previous description of receiving goods is an example of a particular function at a particular organization. Imagine if just one of the mechanical functions in the above list did not occur as it was supposed to, for example, the receiver did not show up to work or trucks could not access the receiving area to unload. Now, consider all the mechanical functions there are in an organization, including routing phone calls and typing up orders correctly. It then becomes easy to understand how pervasive the damage caused by black holes can be. Remember, these are failings management is *unaware* of, and *in volume* these failings can injure organizations. Volume is the key. We are not talking about isolated incidences. We are talking about highly repetitive failings (or less repetitive failings but across a broad spectrum). An organization is a massive network of flows. When some or many of these flows slow or jam, the organization will have a difficult time meeting its objectives. In serious situations, the organization could reach a point where it ceases to function.

Mechanical damage is low-end damage, but it is often broad and repetitive damage that, in the aggregate, has led to the failure of many organizations. According to Statistics Canada, "Almost half of the firms in Canada that go bankrupt do so primarily because of their own deficiencies rather than externally generated problems."[4] What percent of that "almost half" went bankrupt because of low-end mechanical damage that was allowed to chew away at the organization until it was destroyed?

Tiny metal filings that are not flushed away with frequent oil changes can terminate the life of a car engine prematurely as they wear away the engine parts. Camera flashes can terminate the life of a Rembrandt painting prematurely as the tiny packets of energy in the flashes break down the oil paint. Slow moving underground streams can terminate the life of a building prematurely as the building sinks into the cavity left in the sand.

Likewise, if basic repetitive actions are not completed properly, they leave the goals of the organization unrealized, thus allowing black holes to prematurely terminate the life of an organization. Black holes are so vicious and elusive that organizations can disappear without management ever knowing the real reason why.

Structural Damage

If an engineer who is trying to harness the power in a river miscalculates the river's dynamics and constructs a weak retaining wall, that wall might collapse. The water the engineer is trying to divert to generate hydroelectric power will then run off in another direction.

Like rivers, organizations have dynamics that, when understood, can be used to harness the power within the organizations. Black holes alter these dynamics to such an extent that the organization's personnel can no longer harness the power or energy the dynamics represent. Once personnel can no longer channel the power within the dynamics of its organization, the organization cannot achieve its goals with the least effort and at the lowest cost.

As an example of one dynamic, organizations contain a *critical path*. A critical path is the path that materials, documents, thoughts, products, energy, and sometimes bodies flow along. It usually involves a sequence of actions, which limits the speed of flow through the organization. The critical path is the path *limiting the flow*, and restricting increased output. A black hole can

Structural damage caused by black holes includes the following:

1. Imbalances in staffing
2. Uneconomic capital investments
3. Shifts toward unprofitable markets or away from profitable ones
4. Harmful pricing strategies
5. Too great a reliance on one customer or supplier
6. Marketing programs that, by design, will injure the company
7. Continuous production of sub-standard products

alter the critical path without management's awareness of the shift. Without being aware of the shift, management cannot return the organization to its desired critical path, nor can it manage the critical path.

For example, let's say that a purchasing department ordered copper wire that was inconsistent in quality, composition, and size because the purchasers were untrained and made many purchasing errors. Instead of the critical path on the plant floor being the sequence of materials flowing through machines and labourers' hands as the engineers intended, the critical path (the path that limits the flow) has been diverted to product that must be re-worked off-line to meet customer specifications.

Breaks in the flow of work are hard on people. They sap employees of energy, cause them stress, and make them temporarily dull, all of which are forms of structural damage.

Results Damage

Results damage refers to the damage affecting the results that the organization is trying to achieve. Mechanical damage and structural damage will create results damage. As mentioned earlier, the damage caused by black holes is multi-dimensional; therefore, the damage can be explained in many ways and from many angles. One way is to look at mechanical damage. A second way is to look at structural damage. Results damage is a third angle. How you view the damage caused by black holes depends on your interest.

Reduced total output during a given period and reduced output per staff-hour (or per labour-dollar) are examples of results damage. Additional examples are lost sales, increased cost per unit, overhead cost increases, reduced margins, unsatisfactory profits, and increased capital employed (if capital is unnecessarily tied up in unproductive assets). Lawsuits, negative publicity, crime, theft, and waste are also results damage, because they are outcomes that organization management does not want. Failure to reach the organization's goals and objectives is a major type of results damage, as is bankruptcy.

Spin-Off Damage

The spin-off damage caused by black holes in organizations can be monumental, for when the building blocks of organizational functionality are damaged, anything built upon them is likely to be damaged. The decision to promote a product line based heavily on robust *reported* margins, despite narrow *real* margins, could be a bad one.

Organizations with deep pockets have hired the brightest, most experienced minds to work diligently, at considerable cost, to repair the damage caused by black holes. Unfortunately, many have missed entirely the root causes of the organization's dysfunction. This is how insidious, vicious, and tenacious black holes can be. One would be wise to treat them with respect while taking steps to eradicate them.

Downward Spiral

Black holes choke normal operations, are spread by way of chain reactions and compounding, and become root causes of much larger problems. The result is a relentless downward spiral in organizational functionality and survival ability. There are many reasons why organizations deteriorate besides black holes; however, black holes seem to have slipped past most people's radars.

No matter what positive syntropy forces are building the organization up, black hole entropy forces are operating in the background, chewing away at the organization and pulling it down. The information in this book can help begin the process of halting and then reversing this downward spiral, turning it upward and toward the organization's goals.

~ Chapter Summary ~

Mechanical damage and structural damage will lead to results damage. In a world of hyper-competition and increased market risks, it would be wise to handle as many black hole-creating items as one can identify to lessen results damage. It might be necessary to do so, in order to secure the organization's future.

CHAPTER 4

RELIEF FROM RECURRING PROBLEMS

Chapter 4 takes us beyond understanding what a black hole is, and the damage black holes cause, to diffusing black holes. Diffusing black holes is not about entrepreneurial savvy, marketing brilliance, or innovative product development—although those attributes can benefit from black hole removal—but about getting what management has already decided it needs to function properly.

Clear the Burden

Before addressing the *unknown*, we have found it beneficial to address the *known* (or the suspected). Handle the elephant in the room before using a microscope to find further problems and opportunities. Clear the burden of known or suspected problems as best you can, and then move on to the "bottom-up approach" discussed below to search for and then terminate unknown problems. However, some known problems might be plagued by black hole-creating items, in which case such problems will benefit from their removal. Thus, black hole-creating items should sometimes be addressed prior to addressing the larger known problem, if it is safe to delay doing so.

Knowing the amount of burden to clear prior to commencing bottom-up actions is an art, and its application comes with on-site experience. Generally speaking, the following will guide you:

- the easier it is to handle a known problem, the more likely you will handle it before you search for unknown problems
- the more burden you can clear prior to moving on to the "bottom-up approach" the better.

Once the bottom-up approach has commenced, it is not unusual to have to stop it temporarily so that more burden can be cleared.

Bottom-Up Approach Required

In chapter 2, we discussed failures of the micro-level basic building blocks that comprise the foundation of organizations from an organizational functionality perspective. These failures include "incomplete action," "unexpected action," and "disconnected symbiotic actions," among others.

In trying to resolve organizations, we travel to the bottom of organizations to discover numerous failings, such as desirable activities executed improperly, which in turn arise from failures within these basic building blocks. The end of our pursuit is not necessarily discovering that there was a "wrong sequence" type of failure or an "omitted action" type of failure; rather, understanding failures in this way helps us identify and correct higher level problems.

So to remove black holes we travel to the bottom of the organization to look for problems and opportunities at the micro level, after having cleared some of the burden as mentioned above. We travel deep into the middle management "trenches" and supervisory and worker "weeds." We are in search of numerous problems and opportunities, and although we are approaching organizations at a very low level, at least at this point, occasionally we can quickly unearth large problems and opportunities.

Data Gathering

A Basic Premise

To improve an organization's functionality, we have to accept a basic premise:

We know something, but we do not know everything.

This is a premise with which we can all agree, and it underlines the function of data gathering. In other words, before we can fix a problem, we must identify it. And before we can identify it, we must understand the conditions that allowed it to occur.

To get to the root cause of black holes, one must respond to this basic premise by breaking down the data-gathering process into two distinct parts:

- Supplemental questions
- Systematic questions

Supplemental Questions

Each person who undertakes to improve an organization has some knowledge and asks supplemental questions based on that knowledge. For instance, let us consider the improvement to functionality of a parts department. An inquiring person might know enough about the area to ask if the organization has data records concerning frequency of use, stock-outs, damages, shrinkage, space availability, access, security, quality of parts, frequency of failure, and suitability to user needs. A more knowledgeable person, on the other hand, might also ask specific questions about the parts management system software and data input tools, as well as the re-order and stocking process. In other words, the supplemental questions asked are dependent upon the inquiring person's knowledge. Therefore, supplemental questions, while important, can vary dramatically from person to person.

Systematic Questions

We suggest a disciplined systematic approach to observation and data collection because of the elusive nature of black holes. Black holes will continue to evade unless systematically cornered. Additionally, a systematic approach is a good way to prevent one's self from becoming confused in the process.

More importantly, since everyone who undertakes to improve an organization does not know everything, there is a need for a tool—preferably, a simple tool—to help people discover what they do not know about the organization and its problems and opportunities. The systematic questions are designed to be that tool.

For instance, the inquiring person might not know enough to ask about the parts department's lighting or cleanliness. Poor lighting can result in the inaccurate stocking of parts, such as parts being put in the wrong bins. A dirty environment might lead to dealer and customer complaints about grimy parts. Systematic questions are designed to help unearth facts around issues about which the uninformed inquirer might not specifically ask. Tools, or a guiding process, must be used to compensate for a lack of knowledge. In other words, the systematic questions must broaden one's scope of vision.

More on Systematic Questions

A disciplined systematic approach to observation and data collection should include consultation with many employees, in order to gain insight into the actual workings of the organization as it operates today and as it could potentially operate in the future. Not all employees need to be consulted, for some perform the same function. However, the more you consult with employees who perform distinct job functions, the more thorough a black hole-creating item search will be. That being said, when ten employees perform the same function, such as in the estimating department, it can be fruitful to consult more than one, since they will have different experiences and different abilities to observe. For further insight on the value of consulting employees, especially at the lower levels, please refer to the section entitled "The Employees Are the Experts" in chapter 8.

The key is not necessarily to get into the employee's world and see things from his perspective, although that would be helpful. The key is to get the *employee* into his world and encourage him to take a good look at the function he performs, his environment, and how he interacts with his environment, including equipment, materials, fellow employees, customers, suppliers, creditors, government personnel, and others. He should also look at how they interact with him.

It is important for us and for the employees to know why they are employed, so we start the systematic questioning with "Why are you here, from the company's perspective?" or "What company need do you fulfill?" or something similar. This is an important line of questioning, because it connects directly with management's goals and objectives. Asking this question and addressing any uncertainty, or receiving an answer that does not seem to line up with the organization's strategy, can lead to a quick gain for the company. A salesman who thinks the company is paying him to sell (when in reality, the company is paying him to generate contribution margin that can be used to pay overhead and leave a profit) can be more valuable to the organization in a matter of minutes, with a little communication.

The opening systematic questions above focus the employee on where we want him to be focused—on his function. Next, we help the employee observe his function. There are two important facets involved in helping employees observe both black hole-creating items and business opportunities. Both are designed to broaden and deepen an employee's "scope of vision." The two facets include the following:

1. Ask questions in a sequence that approximates the flow of the employee's function.

2. Ask questions that reach all corners of that function.

Let us take a closer look at these two facets.

Flow of function. We sequence the questions in the order that most functions flow. Most functions have inputs, tools, and outputs. Therefore, we ask, "What inputs do you need to accomplish your purpose?" "What tools do you need to accomplish your purpose?" "What are your outputs?" "Who do you give them to and when?"

Reach all corners. In and of themselves, the "flow of function" questions extract a great deal of information that must be duly noted and analyzed. However, the most important reason for asking those questions is not the direct responses they elicit. Rather, it is to direct the employee's attention into all corners of his functions in preparation for answering the last systematic questions.

Last Systematic Questions

When the last systematic questions are asked and just after having viewed his functional terrain, the employee can give a fuller, more valuable answer. The most important questions of all are:

- What problems do you see related to your function, and elsewhere in the company?
- What opportunities do you see related to your function, and elsewhere in the company?

Underlying Principle

This point deserves expansion. We are not simply asking arbitrary questions. The employee will not be prepared to answer the last systematic questions without first applying the initial systematic questioning process.

Please consider the illustration below. If an inquiring person who wants to know how many boats are on the lake simply approaches a bystander and asks him, "How many boats are on the lake?" he will likely receive a fairly automatic reply of "three." That is exactly what the inquirer sees. However, if the inquiring person were to ask the bystander to look at the cottage on the left, then to look at the cottage directly across the lake, and finally, to look at the cottage on the right, the answer received might be "six."

After looking at the areas of the three cottages, the bystander sees a small boat near the dock of each cottage. Therefore, the bystander is able to give a more complete answer. In other words, the inquirer knows something, but not everything. It is therefore the inquirer's job to motivate those with additional knowledge to use what they know to help the inquirer gather data for the decision-making process.

Helpful Mechanism

Have you ever been interrupted and forgotten an important thought? Then in order to recover the lost thought, you revisited thoughts just prior to, and just after, the moment of that important thought? If you have had this experience, the sought-after lost thought likely popped into view again.

A similar type of ability is what we are invoking with this approach. Directing an employee to look in various areas of his function will help the employee observe failings of basic building blocks that have occurred and are in his memory. He will report the failings to you as problems and opportunities that sit immediately *above* those basic building block failings. He will not report to you, "Symbiotic actions were disconnected", but rather, "The distribution manager is very slow at responding to requests for approvals, and that is choking us here in the pricing department."

Readers should not place too much emphasis on failures of basic building blocks. We are more interested in what sits just above those extremely micro-level failures, and further above, as the failures compound upward through the organization and become more destructive. The discussion on basic building blocks is presented to show the ground level of many problems. It also helps readers appreciate the depth we are attempting to peer into, by way of systematic questions, in order to solve problems. One can become too caught up analyzing this micro-level and miss the meaningful problems and opportunities that sit above.

We strove to create a systematic data-gathering methodology that unearths the most black hole-creating items with the least amount of effort. We believe we have accomplished this goal with the simple approach outlined above. These systematic and supplemental questions will unearth numerous black hole-creating items and then allow us to address them.

Sequence of Execution

In practice, the systematic questions above are asked prior to the supplemental questions, because the systematic questions open up the employee's scope of "vision," as explained earlier.

Among the newly discovered problems and opportunities, whatever can be addressed easily is addressed right away. Larger, more complicated issues are logged for further consideration by company management, since more investigation, approval, specialists, or other resources might be required.

Once a few problems and opportunities have been identified and addressed, we continue looking for additional problems and then conducting additional repairs. We repeat this process until there are no more gains for the organization to be economically realized. It is a constant process of "observe" and "repair." For the most part, these are not complicated repairs. As mentioned above, the complicated and more extensive repairs are logged for further consideration by company management.

It is not a situation of conducting a full company-wide review and then addressing the problems. After addressing a few problems, the organization will have shifted so much that the balance of the recommendations will diminish in usefulness. Therefore, reviewing must not get too far ahead of repairing. Organizations are ratcheted up on a controllable gradient, leaving the organization's management in control of the process at all times. A worthy systematic approach to observation and data collection in the presence of a black hole will "kick up" numerous problems and opportunities. Anyone performing this task will become overwhelmed if he does not constantly reduce the number of unaddressed problems and opportunities by handling some of them.

Why take a bottom-up approach?

1. It leads to the termination of root causes yet leaves the goodness intact.
2. Increased transparency will unearth previously hidden problems and opportunities.
3. It is better to address some larger problems and opportunities after the lower-level shifting has occurred, if it is safe to delay resolving them, because changes made at the bottom alter their anatomy.
4. It gives the organization some quick gains.

After a significant amount of systematic observation and data collection has been performed and subsequent basic repairs have been made, one can look at the overall data, including the larger potential problems and opportunities that were logged but not investigated further. One does this to identify additional large problems and opportunities with the benefit of having traveled through several departments, or the entire organization, and with the benefit of greater organizational transparency. One steps back and looks at the "big picture." At this point, one might discover that on the day the budget was approved, it was physically impossible to achieve it, or that the ambitions of the marketing department do not align to the constraints of the plant.

The above sounds so basic and simple, and it is, and that is the point of this book. Organizations have drifted away from the basics and this has allowed problems to form. Often substantial problems. Occasionally terminal problems.

Here again, we see the importance of understanding key dynamics of organizations. It is fruitful to understand such dynamics because they lead to the resolution of larger, more difficult, and often hitherto unknown problems.

Terminating Root Causes

When problems are unearthed, no matter what temporary measures one puts in place to stop the "bleeding," eventually one must terminate the root causes. To do so, one should view root causes at several levels of abstraction but deal with them at a workable level. By workable, I mean at a level that can lead to a resolution. As an example:

Indicator: Accounts receivable sub-ledger is ballooning but sales are not.

Problem: Customers are not paying invoices.

    1st-level cause: Prices on invoices are frequently wrong.

    2nd-level cause: Data-entry person is making keying errors.

    3rd-level cause: No edit checks are built into data-entry software.

    4th-level cause: IT manager is incompetent.

    5th-level cause: President is incompetent for hiring the IT manager and for not replacing him.

In this example, the third-level cause—"No edit checks are built into data-entry software"—is the level we are interested in, because it is the first workable level: "We determine that a lack of edit checks is the root cause of customers' failure to pay invoices."

"Prices on invoices are frequently wrong" is not a level at which you can terminate the root causes because you do not know why the prices are wrong. And "Data entry person is making keying errors" is not a workable level either, because human error will always be present in high-volume, repetitive tasks—although you should still give this area some attention. "IT manager is incompetent" is not a workable level, because you cannot replace a manager every time something small goes wrong. Nor should you replace a president so quickly.

If you simply try to tackle the undesirable result—"Accounts receivable sub-ledger is ballooning but sales are not"—you might not find the root cause of the problem. Pressuring good paying customers to pay even earlier, to make up for the seriously delinquent customers, temporarily lowers the accounts receivable sub-ledger balance, but it does not terminate the cause of the problem.

Often, you can find the root cause of the undesirable result much earlier in the process. This is especially important to know, given that many root causes of larger problems do not appear to be significant and therefore are not tracked down, or terminated. The fact that these incidents, despite appearing insignificant, are high-volume and *repetitive* allows them to grow and destroy organizations. Therefore, they warrant our attention.

Insisting that area managers forward price overrides to the pricing department before (or at the same time as) they forward them to customers is not as glamorous as deciding to hedge the foreign loan. However, this process—as well as fifteen other similar, repetitive tasks that have broken down—has the potential to be just as destructive as hedging incorrectly.

An Analogy

A snake that lunges at a person from within a pile of rubbish stacked against the barn would not have been so threatening if one had removed the pile, exposing the snake as it lay coiled and on the bare earth. As it is with snakes and rubbish, so it is with problems and clogged organizations. The resolution to the two problems is the same: transparency. Remove the rubbish, piece by piece, thereby removing the places where snakes can hide. Likewise, remove the backlogs, the breaks, the disconnects, and the conflicting—possibly even destructive—policies. Remove poor data integrity and uncertainty, bit by bit, like peeling an onion. Do this until the area becomes totally transparent and you have eliminated the places where big problems can hide.

As the rubbish is removed, piece by piece, some snakes will scatter and flee and other snakes will be captured and be rendered harmless. Likewise, as you remove the items clogging an organization, one by one, some large problems will disperse naturally and other large problems will be found and diffused as their root causes are terminated.

Align the Thought Processes

There is a fine line of intention running through most organizations—management's intention. The intention could be to deliver fresh bread on time, to keep customer internet services running with less than two hours of down time each year, or to install fireplaces within 72 hours of the customer placing an order.

As employees pay attention to the fine line of intention running through the organization, they begin to align their thought processes to those of the organization, and in turn, they align their actions. In this way, the organization begins to ratchet upward on a controllable gradient. When this line of thinking is in play, you can see the root causes of problems for what they are—destructive impediments to the long-term goals, prosperity, and survival of the organization. With that as a guiding principle, organizations become more open and willing to terminate the root causes of problems.

~ Chapter Summary ~

To address black holes, one uses a bottom-up gradient approach that keeps organization management in control of the process—a process of toggling between observing and repairing. Faced with an unwanted result, one has to do some digging to find the root cause. Root causes can take on almost any form and must be terminated eventually. The key is to dig deep enough, leading to the termination of both the undesirable result linked to the root cause and the root cause itself.

CHAPTER 5

THE SIMPLICITY OF IT ALL

The story of black holes in organizations is a sad one because of the slow but steady destruction they cause. However, it is also sad because black holes receive such little attention. Activities executed by people are not as stable and consistent as computer programs. People err. People have limitations. However addressing deficiencies in activities, black hole-creating items, might be as important as correctly programming company payroll.

The Simplicity of the Problem

As you read this book and scan appendix A, "What Do Black Holes Look Like?" you will find that the causes of black holes are not complicated. The concepts, the root causes of black holes, make good common sense. In fact, the truths are so simple they are *almost* funny at times. Unfortunately, the destruction of an organization is no laughing matter.

It is this simplicity that camouflages the sinister nature of black holes. Too often, managers fall into the trap of looking for complexity because they cannot believe that the obvious, simple situations, *in volume*, could be the root causes of such serious and compounding negative results.

The Simplicity of the Solution

As with the placer gold miners of old, eradicating black holes all starts with people rolling up their sleeves, willing to get a little dirty and bruised, and traveling down the organization to the bedrock to harvest organizational gains. The placer miners knew where to find gold nuggets and grains of gold—on the bedrock, buried under a burden of soil and gravel. They knew why the gold was there—it could sink no further. That is why bedrock, sometimes beneath many feet of soil and gravel, was the target of the placer gold miners.

As it was with the placer gold miners, so it should be with organizations. Organizations have bedrock. One must get to it to find the "golden opportunities that lie beneath." One unearths and then terminates the previously hidden disconnects and breaks found at the lower levels which are causing black holes to form. Then the process of rolling up the organization and discovering new and greater problems and opportunities can begin.

It is simple, in theory, and thus the title of this chapter, "The Simplicity of It All," but it takes a lot of digging and effort to eradicate black holes. Once you are there, the entire journey will prove to be worthwhile.

~ Chapter Summary ~

Black holes have been allowed to form and persist because their simplicity has misled both management and assisting consultants as to their destructive power. Luckily, just as simplicity is the hallmark of black hole-creating items, simplicity is also the hallmark of their discovery and subsequent eradication.

Despite simplicity, the eradication of black holes requires significant effort.

CHAPTER 6

THE PRIZE

If one ventures to streamline an organization, he ventures to streamline toward something. Streamlining is the process of making the best use of an organization's resources in pursuit of its goals, one of which should be long-term survival and prosperity. However, real gains in this direction may be different from reported gains.

Real Gains

Anyone who is trying to improve the long-term survival and prosperity of an organization should strive to attain *real gains*.

Inevitably, the process of resolving black holes will unearth inaccurate financial reports. The inaccurate financial reports might have arisen out of under-staffing, the sudden shift in the business that can happen after a big-change event, the loss of key report-compiling employees, carelessness, incompetence, intent to deceive, or outright fraud. Regardless of their origin, the *real* financial position and the *perceived* financial position of the organization are likely to be different the day that one begins to address a black hole. Such is the nature of black holes. Real gains are crucial to the survival of an organization, reported gains less so.

Numerous Opportunities

It is always wise to relieve an organization of black hole-creating items. Below are some of the more critical times to do so:

- When a vacuum in procedures forms for any of a number of reasons, such as when an organization races ahead to beat the competition and the various departments have trouble keeping up
- When breaks or confusion occur *after* structural change, such as a merger, sell-off, de-layering, reorganization, or computer conversion
- *Prior to* structural change, such as a merger, sell-off, de-layering, reorganization, or computer conversion (to better prepare the organization for absorbing the upcoming changes)
- After an organization matures and becomes lethargic
- When management senses "smoke" in one of its many forms, such as conflicting data, incomprehensible data, confusion about an area of the organization, or operational irregularities
- When the organization is experiencing a large number of customer or supplier complaints
- When new management arrives and wants to know the organization's current condition and its potential
- When existing management wants to know if the organization is operating at the level at which it believes the organization to be operating
- When management is feeling pain because of numerous internal problems

Substantial Gains

If an organization were to organize and understand itself, and if it had everyone working together, then maybe it would be more *predictable*, and maybe *less energy* would be required to deliver the goods. This would translate into more energy to develop and launch a new product line without adding staff. Or perhaps the organization could divest some capital assets that were no longer required. Either option would increase the return on investment and improve cash flow. Or creative juices might flourish in a saner environment. Certainly, risk would be reduced.

Imagine if all or the vast majority of the black hole-creating items were terminated. What would the organization look like then? What higher level opportunities and problems would then be *visible*? Imagine how creative the executive team could become and the *sound strategies* it could develop, once it clearly saw the organization it had been entrusted to steward. Furthermore, the executive team would have a better handle on the organization's financial, human, machinery, and equipment resources. Imagine how *effective* management could be when the organization is cleared of its burden and is functionally aligned. The potential for such an organization to reach its goals, including long-term survival and prosperity, would increase dramatically.

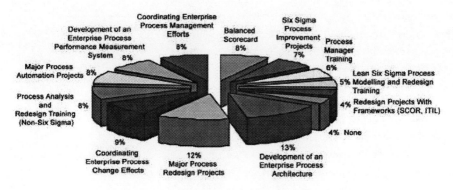

Activities in which companies were engaged in 2005

Reproduced by permission from *The State of Business Process Management, 2006, fig. 26.*[5]

Often when management introduces business process improvement initiatives, they assume basic micro-level organizational functionality is not impaired, and then proceed to layer change upon the organization. Celia Wolf and Paul Harmon at Business Process Trends[6] have performed extensive work analyzing the business process improvement sector. Some of their findings are depicted in the above chart. How many of the activities in the above chart could have benefited from the removal of black hole-creating items before commencing those activities? How much additional value would these activities have yielded, how much money could have been saved, or how much risk could have been reduced by eliminating or at least lessening a black hole prior to commencing such activities and other management initiatives?

Eradicating black holes increases badly needed transparency, reduces risk, increases efficiency and effectiveness, increases control, and results in a host of other generic benefits; however, the gains available are as varied as the goals of organizations. In pursuit of these gains, organizations must remove black holes in order for true streamlining or other organizational betterment initiatives to succeed. Skyscrapers and three-story office buildings alike need sound foundations.

Likewise, organizations need sound foundations, of which effective organizational functionality is an integral part.

Competition and market demands, in the form of quality and price tolerance, will dictate whether an organization in a particular industry can survive and prosper with a significant black hole in its midst. Organizations across an industry that individually suffer from their own black holes actually keep one another in business. If any one of these organizations cleared their black holes, that organization could have a significant competitive advantage.

Reducing black holes in organizations is, or at least should be, an *early* defensive strategy against potential troubles. Unfortunately for too many organizations, management considers it a *late in the game* defensive strategy, i.e., to be used only when the pain threshold has been exceeded, if indeed they consider black holes at all. You can avoid significant trouble by addressing black holes in organizations very early on, before they have an opportunity to take root and seriously harm the organization, or better yet, before they have had a chance to form.

> Often substantial gains can be realized by removing black hole-creating items prior to commencing management initiatives.

~ Chapter Summary ~

Real gains are the only gains worth pursuing, and one can expect substantial real gains if organizations remove their significant black holes. By terminating black hole-creating items, we increase transparency, efficiency and effectiveness, and build a base for better execution, better decision making, and accurate reporting.

Among other benefits, increased transparency will help management to discover whether the organization is operating at the level which it thinks it is operating at, or far below—and the earlier this is known the better.

CHAPTER 7

THE ULTIMATE PRICE TO PAY

Would boards of directors, shareholders, employees, pensioners, credit rating agencies, and creditors be tolerant of managers who ignored black holes that could result in multi-million dollar write-offs?

Mergers, sell-offs, acquisitions, re-engineering, workflow implementations, computer conversions, modeling, and re-modeling definitely have their places but how much value is left on the table, how much additional risk is assumed, by pursuing one or more of these avenues without first addressing the organization's black holes?

From experience, we know the answer. An astounding amount of value is left on the table, and an astounding amount of risk is assumed, when black holes remain undetected and unaddressed.

Any way we look at it, addressing black hole-creating items has a significant payoff; ignoring them is a path to ruin.

Ignoring black hole-creating items causes damage to organizations in at least two ways: (1) left unattended, they create more black hole-creating items in a chain reaction; and (2) over time the same black hole-creating items will cause mechanical damage, structural damage, and of course, results damage as mentioned earlier. The two charts below depict exponential damage levels that can occur in organizations because of an increasing number of black hole-creating items (table 7.1, "Road to Ruin—A") and their effect over time (table 7.2, "Road to Ruin—B"). When the organization reaches the point where it can no longer support a black hole, it becomes insolvent.

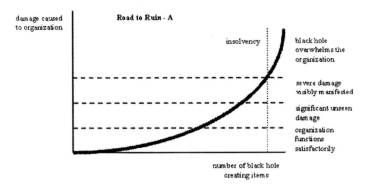

Table 7.1, Road to Ruin—A

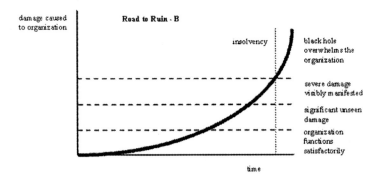

Table 7.2, Road to Ruin—B

~ **Chapter Summary** ~

The ultimate price to pay for ignoring a black hole in an organization is corporate bankruptcy.

PART II

OTHER CONSIDERATIONS

CHAPTER 8

THE EMPLOYEE CONNECTION

Almost all black hole-creating items involve non-executive employees, therefore chapter 8 will expand on the relationship between these employees and black holes. To start, employees always pay for unresolved black holes, because working in the vicinity of a black hole means working in a stressful, high-risk, and chaotic environment.

The Employees Are the Experts

If you are traveling to an unfamiliar geographic location that lies off the beaten trail and you want to know directions, you ask the locals, especially if the location is sparsely populated and not on any map.

Likewise, when one wants directions on a procedure, or a better understanding of the organization's makeup, one travels down the organization into the middle-management "trenches" and into the supervisory and worker "weeds". One travels there to ask the "locals," those familiar with that part of the organization, because they work there every day. For what is written in manuals might be different from what is practiced today.

The employees are the experts on how the organization *currently* functions. Management is the strategist, the regulator, the provider of basic tools and training, the motivator, and the supplier of the factors of production and of the organization's dream and direction.

Even someone who knows nothing about an organization can help improve its functionality by obtaining data from employees, analyzing the facts surrounding that data, drawing conclusions based on that data, and then acting.

In many instances, the long forgotten clerk is the individual holding the organization together—until he or she finds other employment, is transferred elsewhere, retires, or collapses. There goes your talent pool. There goes your collective ingenuity.

Beyond the current situation, there is the future to consider, one in which employees can supply vital input.

Of course, employees will, at times, give wrong or misleading answers to questions or offer up valueless ideas, as do we all. Sorting

> Three thousand employees watching vigilantly over the organization make up the team that will carry the organization into the future. However, if neglected, they become a wasting force-untapped and unfulfilled and in a state of decay, but still collecting their paychecks.

through the vast sea of ideas offered up by employees and finding (as well as crediting and rewarding) the gems—those ideas that are of value to the organization—is a management task.

It is up to management to accept or reject ideas, and to foster an environment where people are encouraged to offer additional ideas. Wise management is thankful that ideas are offered up, even when they have to reject them. The alternative is a thought vacuum, and vacuums are deadly. "The employees are the experts" does not mean they are the ultimate decision makers—management retains that responsibility. However, it does mean they possess abundant organizational survival power.

Ignoring the concept "the employees are the experts" can hinder an organization that must compete in the marketplace for sales and profits. Conversely, grasping this concept and acting upon it will give an organization a marked edge over those organizations that do not. Steelmaker Dofasco Inc. capitalized on this concept, as reflected in its credo, "Our product is steel. Our strength is people."

New Boss

Your new boss grew up in a small town. Aspiring to become an executive of a large corporation, he went to university and received an MBA. Now, this highly educated individual is your boss. Given that the employees are the experts, if your new boss does not realize there is a great deal of collective knowledge embedded in them, he will likely become a part of a black hole creation, since one person alone cannot know the entire complexity of an organization.

Furthermore, if *anyone*—employee or otherwise—who is trying to improve the organization's functionality does not realize there is a great deal of collective knowledge embedded in the organization's employees, he will likely cause more breaks, create a black hole, or exacerbate an existing one. By failing to grasp a few such organizational dynamics, such people work at cross-purposes—against rather than with the organization.

How does one swim across a fast-moving river? One does not swim straight across. One swims diagonally, in the direction of the river flow, not against it. To improve an organization's functionality, one uses the dynamics of the organization to their best advantage. Fighting the river is unwise. Likewise, fighting the dynamics of the organization is unwise. One can leverage organizations, including the employee base, in the same way a swimmer leverages the current of a fast-flowing river.

~ **Chapter Summary** ~

Employees possess valuable information necessary for the smooth operation of an organization. Anyone trying to improve organizational functionality, including both internal management and external consultants, would be wise to tap into it. This valuable information is not necessarily dispersed evenly among employees, nor is it necessarily complete, nor always readily accessible without effort. It does, however, remain valuable.

CHAPTER 9

CORPORATE GOVERNANCE

When one hears of corporate governance, one likely envisions the very top of organizations: boardrooms, directors, officers, share issues, minutes, policies, annual and special meetings, audit committees, and corporate seals.

While directors and officers are heavily involved in corporate governance, and are in fact legally responsible for it, the actual activities of corporate governance extend well below the executive offices.

Preserving the Continuity of the Business

Chartered Secretaries Canada has prepared its *Index of Good Governance Guides* (see appendix B, "Good Governance Guides") to help guide its members and others toward good organizational governance. The first sentence of section 4.3 "Business Continuity Planning/Disaster Recovery," states:

> As a matter of good governance and risk management your organization should anticipate the unexpected and plan to preserve the continuity of the business while minimizing disruption to service in situations involving calamity or crisis.[7]

This is applicable to any corporation in North America and, for the most part, the world over.

An organization that is healthy, from an organizational functionality point of view, can better absorb the unexpected because the organization's resources are not severely stressed nor overloaded from trying to cope with breaks in otherwise routine procedures. On the other hand, an organization burdened with a black hole is already exerting excess energy while trying to function on a day-to-day basis. The additional burden of a "calamity or crisis" can easily jeopardize the "continuity of the business." This concept of "absorption"—an organization's ability to weather a calamity—is an important concept for the survival of organizations.

Executives responsible for corporate governance often spend much time, money, and energy on analyzing external threats. The potential damage caused by external threats can be reduced if the threats can be absorbed or cordoned off. One drop of sulfuric acid dropped into a glass of water can be absorbed by the water and therefore will not create a noticeable reaction. Half a glass of sulfuric acid dropped into half a glass of water can cause a violent, potentially dangerous, and even lethal reaction. It is the same with organizations and external threats.

One way to reduce external threats is to steel the organization internally by diffusing black holes.

Need for Transparency

Section 6 of Chartered Secretaries Canada's *Index of Good Governance Guides* is titled "Transparency." Black holes remove transparency from organizations. Their ability to exist unseen has allowed them to fester largely unheeded in organizations throughout the world.

Black holes remove transparency through broken procedures, loss of data integrity, the creation of informal systems that become incubators for crime, incorrect or incomplete work, withered responsibility (whereby employees withdraw and no longer maintain a vigilant eye for internal and external threats to the organization), and many more negative activities. You can find expanded commentary on this subject in appendix A, "What Do Black Holes Look Like?"

Sound Risk Management

Section 6.3 of Chartered Secretaries Canada's *Index of Good Governance Guides,* "Risk Management", lists some benefits of sound risk management, including "improved resource allocation," "maintenance of the integrity of internal controls," and "improved and more informed decision making." Black holes hinder these goals. They waste resources. They make it difficult, and at times impossible, to perform basic internal business controls, because the data required is not aligned with the control processes. Black holes render informed decision making impossible. Instead, decisions are based on false, omitted, erroneous, or misleading data.

~ Chapter Summary ~

Clearly, black holes harm organizations. Black holes severely impede an organization's goals and threaten its long-term survival and prosperity. Black holes are a corporate governance risk and must be addressed.

CHAPTER 108

EXTERIOR ATTEMPTS TO PREDICT ORGANIZATION FAILURE

Most organizations fail—meaning they terminate involuntarily—for a simple reason. Cash out exceeds cash in. Soon there is no cash, just great debt, and creditor patience wears thin.

What causes cash out to exceed cash in? There are a number of "reasons." Below are some of them, with potential root causes in brackets:

1. Markets are not willing to pay what it costs the company to produce a product or deliver a service (possibly because a black hole drives up costs).

2. Markets do not know about the availability of the product or service and therefore do not purchase it (possibly because a black hole has caused internal confusion or misalignment).

3. Competition sells a similar product for more and convinces markets to buy from them (possibly because a black hole has eaten away at funds intended for the sales and marketing budget).

4. Embezzlement and other forms of theft plague the company (possibly because a black hole hides these activities).

5. Cash is squandered on non-essential items, including excessive shareholder draws (possibly because a black hole has reduced the transparency of the true cash situation).

Creditors, large shareholders, auditors, regulators, bond raters, researchers, government officials, and others use business-failure prediction models to determine the health of companies.

Several experts have developed a number of business-failure prediction models over the years to help predict company failure[9]. You can apply these models if accurate and timely data can be obtained. Most of these models are technical works that make for an enlightening read, but as I will outline and despite their value, there are several problems with the use of business-failure prediction models.

Problems with Prediction Models

Bankruptcy and solvency specialist Kip E. Jones, CPA, states the following: "While continuing research has been ongoing for almost thirty years, it is interesting to note that **no unified well-specified theory of how and why corporations fail has yet been developed.**"[10] Senior executives should be aware of the inherent problems with organization-failure prediction models. Below, I outline some of these problems.[11]

1. Many assumptions have to be made when interpreting information, including the methods of accounting that have been used. Any limitations in the accounting data used will also affect the models.

2. Problems in valuing the equity in private companies (because there is no market for the shares) may make it difficult to apply some aspects of certain models.

3. The data used in business-failure prediction models comes largely from published accounts, which may be out of date, and therefore reflects the past. For predictability purposes, any relationships found may or may not hold good in future.

4. The prediction models monitor some events which surface so late in the business-failure process that they have little or no usefulness from a resolution perspective.

5. Prediction models take little or no account of economic conditions, either during the past period on which they are based or in terms of the future that they are trying to forecast.

6. Companies may manipulate the measures used in the models to prevent predictions of failure. Internal management are often masters at disguising inherent problems. Just as a bankrupt person postpones bankruptcy by misleading creditors in an attempt to avoid the pain, management often fools outsiders in an attempt to avoid the pain. This delusion often continues until the internal rot and damage is so severe that the company implodes.

To that list, we can add "business models change." At times, they change dramatically, as seen with the global and explosive use of high-risk, unregulated, unlisted, non-standardized financial derivatives. These derivatives have significant systemic and counter-party risk. They are instruments whose ability to perform depends on the strength of the balance sheet of the *loser* in the transaction. They have no clearinghouse guarantee and lack transparency, even to the management of the derivative-owning organization.[12,13] In my opinion, globally, derivatives are a disaster waiting to happen. Their Achilles' heel is counter-party risk, which has not been properly factored into the global derivatives pyramid. We can conclude, among other things, that even global financial systems are not immune to black holes.

Add Black Holes

There is one more reason why business-failure prediction models often fail—black holes. Given what is shown in appendix A, "What Do Black Holes Look Like?" it is obvious why these approaches, or models, fail at times to predict the failure of organizations. These models rely on data that is too distant from many of the actual problems causing the failure. *They are too distant in "mechanics" and in "time".* Black holes are not the only reason that organizations deteriorate; however, when a black hole *is* the reason, or is a major contributor, traditional late-in-the-chain prediction models will be of little value if the goal is to save the organization.

Too Distant in Mechanics

Mechanical handlings include manually completing documents, gathering documents (such as work orders), entering data into a computer, programming a report, running the program to group data with other data, and further aggregating data on a worksheet or in one's head. "Too distant in mechanics" means there are several mechanical handlings of the data, between the actual events and the point that the data is ready to be used to draw conclusions within a business failure prediction model.

When many mechanical handlings are required, the problem is that they increase the chance for valuable information to be lost, and they increase the likelihood of error. For example, when additional costs are incurred for plant overtime because raw materials are received late, the additional cost is lumped into the weekly pay of each labourer who worked overtime, and then it is further grouped into direct labour. Only the premium is allocated to overhead. In most prediction models, this additional expense simply shows up as a cost for direct labour—without a reason. Depending on the model used, even the fact that additional expenses were put toward direct labour might become lost as aggregate numbers are compiled.

Such grouping increases the likelihood for management to make generalizations that are purged of valuable data, resulting in the failure to utilize information valuable to business failure prediction. Will the problem of material shortages be resolved and result in increased margins and improved ratios? On the other hand, a positive, unrelated event the following month, such as producing a different product mix that has better margins on average, can give the mistaken appearance that the material receipts problem was handled. Or the material receipts problem might have been handled, but a new problem hurts margins and ratios, this time giving the mistaken appearance that the material receipts problem is chronic and has not been resolved.

Too Distant in Time

The term "too distant in time" includes delays in reporting, for example, the events of January 6 until the first-quarter financial statements are published in May. A worse situation would be looking at data to spot trends over a period that will likely extend well beyond a year, and likely several years, because annual reports sometimes include entries that are not booked quarterly. A situation occurring over one or two periods does not make a trend because there are not enough data points to establish a trend, therefore a long time horizon is required. All the while, the organization is incurring damage.

Using trend analysis, one misses the beginning of the trend, making it difficult for one to conclude and take action at this critical moment, when the trend is forming. Root causes are not sought in a timely manner when business-failure prediction models rely on trends, because the trends are not yet seen as trends, or they are not sought at all. Subsequently, instead of laser-precision minor repairs being conducted on a timely basis at the lower levels of the organization, the organization applies a Herculean effort at a much later point in time to get the organization back on track. This approach is successful at times, but it is costly and usually unnecessary.

Seeking Root Causes

Some business-failure prediction models do seek out root causes at some level. The Institute of Chartered Accountants in England and Wales, for example, identified a number of factors that put continuity into question.[14]

1. Loss of key management and staff
2. Significantly higher stock levels, without the apparent source of finance to pay for them
3. Regular work stoppages and labour disputes
4. Dependence on a single product or project
5. Dependence on a single supplier, or a large customer
6. Outstanding legal proceedings
7. Political risks
8. Technical obsolescence
9. Loss of a major franchise or patent
10. History of poor performance within the industry

To consider black holes in organizations when attempting to predict business failure is to seek out root causes of at least one of the significant reasons for business failure: *black hole-creating items disrupt organizational functionality.*

The Gap Can Be Narrowed

To consider black holes in organizations, when attempting to predict business failure, is to narrow the gaps in "mechanics" and "time." However, to narrow these gaps, one must expend effort on site—within an organization—working through black hole-creating items. Or one must at least have access to this type of documentation (which is available to local management, internal boards of directors, and parent companies) and receive it on a timely basis.

~ **Chapter Summary** ~

Internally, company management and controlling shareholders can greatly benefit from black hole knowledge. An internal understanding of an organization's black holes will complement business-failure prediction models and increase management's ability to minimize threats to the organization.

Externally, black holes play a large role in the general difficulty in predicting company failure.

PART III

THE FUTURE

CHAPTER 11

A LEAP FORWARD

Sometimes, to *see*, one must step back from what one is looking at. Sir John Templeton, one of the world's most successful money managers, walked away from Wall Street and set up an office in the Bahamas to distance himself from the noise and influence of Wall Street.[15] When one is deeply entrenched in the old way, or when one mirrors or uses many fragments of the old way to build a new way, one usually limits his ability to build a better way. It is true that most gains in society are incremental and progress along a narrow path, building marginally upon a vast amount of data in that field. However, the big leaps are usually not the result of such evolution. They tend to be "eureka" moments of discovery involving huge, fruitful gaps between those frequent but narrow strings of incremental gains.

Viewing life or business using the three thinking tools below, one can create remarkably beneficial insights that diverge from traditional thinking:

1. Start with a *blank slate*. Delete all previous conclusions about what you are looking at, as they are probably loaded with ingrained opinion, faulty logic, deception, bad judgment, propaganda, errors, bad habits, and misrepresentation.

2. Use your *observation* ability to observe the raw data.

3. Apply your ability to *reason*, deduce, and conclude.

This thought pattern results in positive leaps forward. In particular, this way of thinking helped me identify the nature of black holes in organizations and assisted in the development of a technology used to eradicate black holes from organizations.

Of the three thought tools, the first is the most difficult one to use as one is drawn into old thought patterns, because that is the path of least effort, pulling a person away from potential insight. Hollow promises and clichéd mantras, such as "work smarter, not harder" and "best practices" are admirable goals, but they are too often spouted as solutions without much substance to back them up. Why limit an organization to *copying* the current best instead of *thinking* how to be better than they are?

Observations

No matter who I was working with at the time, we had to reach a frame of mind where we could start with a blank slate. Then we were able to observe the raw data and apply our ability to reason, deduce, and conclude from a fresh perspective. In doing so, we found a significant source of confusion, recurring problems, over-worked conditions, fire-fighting, inaccurate reports, wrong conclusions, frustration, and threats to survival that are so easy to observe in many organizations. We also found the source of many deteriorated financial positions of organizations including corporate bankruptcies. And we found the source of many less dire though undesirable situations, such as lost efficiencies and increased labour costs.

We found the anatomy of black holes: breaks, dropped balls, disconnects, incomplete work, inconsistencies, uncorrected errors, lack of data integrity, misalignment, interrupted information flows, interrupted idea flows, interrupted personnel and material flows, neglect, and maliciousness. We found a whole host of undesirable activities and a lack of desirable activities at the micro level, unknown to management, many of which had earlier root causes.

Looking at the organization from the blank slate point of view, we also saw the following:

1. How organizations could be viewed to help improve functionality
2. How thought processes and workflow could be viewed to give gains to organizations
3. Previously hidden reasons for organizational failures
4. Where recurring breakdowns occur

5. How one part of an organization compensates for other parts of the organization in times of crisis

6. How "pockets" form in organizations

7. Impediments to the success of technological implementation and innovation

8. Impediments to the success of various organizational betterment methodologies

9. Why data valuable to management remained occluded

10. How one could begin to locate the root causes of all this turmoil

Conclusions

The blank slate approach, applied on site and deep within the bellies of organizations under stress and pressure, began to yield results. By observing raw data, unencumbered by conventional wisdom, we started to unearth the findings that now form part of Corporate Streamlining Technology, some of which have been incorporated into this book.

Whether or not our observations were new, when brought together they helped us form strong conclusions:

1. Black holes exist.

2. Black holes can be defined (see chapter 1).

3. Black holes harm organizations and hurt shareholders, directors, employees, and other stakeholders.

4. Black holes can be eradicated (see chapter 4).

Academia

Black holes require more attention than a handful of streamliners can give, for the world is large and black holes are many. Colleges, universities, and professional bodies would greatly assist organizations if they allocated part of their curriculum to this badly neglected area. Then black holes would no longer have a place to hide. Organization executives, managers, and frontline employees would benefit from being fluent in black hole theory. Any assistance academic institutions could give in this field would be beneficial.

~ **Chapter Summary** ~

There was definitely an area of organizations that had been overlooked-understandably so, because it was well hidden. Although buried beneath an almost mundane simplicity, black holes in organizations are nonetheless real. Powerful, ruthless, destructive, yet stealth-like in nature, the great unknown *black holes in organizations, and black hole-creating items,* became known.

It is time to eradicate the black holes that plague organizations. Once that is done, organizations can get on with the job of being the best they can be and the most innovative, productive, functional, and profitable they can be.

After all, isn't that what they set out to be in the first place?

CHAPTER 12

THE FUTURE OF ORGANIZATIONS

The pendulum between hands-on daily business activities and top management strategy and governance has gradually swung to the latter at the expense of the former. This has caused gaping holes to form in some organizations. These holes can easily be discovered and then addressed by swinging the pendulum toward the middle. Outlined below is my vision of the future.

Management Tool

As management understands black holes and realizes that they can be diffused, they will no longer tolerate them, for who would tolerate a thorn at the bottom of his foot when he could simply remove it?

It will be standard operating procedure to run a *micro-level* "black hole check" prior to undertaking a management initiative to ensure the organization is organized and strong enough to implement the initiative successfully, or at least to increase the chance of its success. Running a "black hole check" prior to a significant information technology initiative, for example, will become so standard that failing to do so will put the project's adherents at risk. Information technology professionals are already performing some of this work along these lines. There are benefits to doing more.

Diffusing black holes need not be limited to upcoming information technology projects. Adding a new product line, changing locations, merging with another organization, changing suppliers, reworking price models, re-negotiating distributor agreements, conducting a supply chain review, and many other management initiatives can benefit from the reduction of black holes. Occasionally, initiatives will cause the formation of black holes, in which case a "black hole check" should also be conducted *after* implementation of an initiative.

Management will come to know the benefit of diffusing black holes and will consider such action a valuable management tool for numerous circumstances. An organization free of black holes will also give management peace of mind therefore management will ensure this by periodically initiating a search for them, even when no *visible* indicators of one are present. Large organizations will hire an in-house compliance officer to perpetually search for black hole-creating items and eradicate them.

Compliance Officer

A compliance officer helps to hold the form of the organization as it moves forward. There will come a day in the future of large organizations when failing to hire a compliance officer will be perceived as a serious governance shortfall. This perception will be a natural outcome of organization personnel grasping the existence and the character of black holes and its subsequent damage, then ridding the organization of the black holes. They will never want one to surface again. Pain has that effect.

After reflecting on the damage a black hole has caused and the effort it took to eradicate the black hole, management teams will look for solutions to stifle the recurrence of black holes. One strong restraint will be a well-trained compliance officer.

Compliance officers are not new to organizations. They have existed for decades to ensure organizations comply with contracts and government and industry regulations. Recently, the Society of Corporate Compliance and Ethics, headquartered in Minneapolis, Minnesota, began offering Certified Compliance and Ethics Professional certification (http://www.corporatecompliance.org). An extract from their Web site reads, "The CCEP is a professional with knowledge of relevant regulations and expertise in compliance processes sufficient to assist corporate industries to understand and address legal obligations, and promote organizational integrity through the operation of effective compliance programs."

However, I am proposing a compliance officer who will not have his attention riveted on government and other regulatory rules, but rather on organizational functionality. Specifically, this officer will maintain an eagle eye, searching for black hole-creating items so that organizations operate *as management intended*. He will continuously and systematically comb through the organization searching for black hole-creating items and then ensure they are terminated early. He will have his hands full in some organizations, as entropy in various forms tries to exert itself over syntropy and overwhelm the organization. Syntropy and entropy, in constant battle within organizations, will be a thoroughly understood concept in future organizations. Management will ensure they apply more syntropy to the organization than entropy impinges upon it and they will do this almost as a matter of routine. Once a competent compliance officer and his team are in place and are fully supported by responsible top management, then internally generated cycles of "everything is fine" followed by "breath-taking plunges" will end, eliminating the threat to the organization's survival before black holes reach critical mass.

Interface with Other Methods

Future organizations will understand the benefits of addressing black holes. Additionally, they will understand how compatible and how necessary it is to lessen the power of black holes with the many other methodologies they employ. Six Sigma, SCOR, Lean, as well as many small-shop and international general practitioners can benefit from the work of professionals who specialize in identifying and handling black hole-creating items. Lessening black holes will increase the success of their own projects, and in time they will come to know this. Similarly, wise black hole specialists will know when to pass the baton on to various other well-trained specialists, consequently allowing themselves time to concentrate on black holes and giving them the attention they demand. Once they have unearthed problems of specialization or uniqueness and passed the baton to other specialists, black hole specialists will gain respect within their industry and among the business-improvement community. The business-improvement community will come to know that black hole specialists are "safe" and are not merely practitioners who wish to encroach far beyond their area of expertise. In this way, the entire business-improvement community will become stronger, and customer organizations will win.

~ Chapter Summary ~

Many management teams have drifted away from hands-on basic activities, and this has allowed black holes to form. The pendulum can now swing toward a balance between "top end strategy and decision making" and "micro-level execution." Once management understands that black holes hamper corporate governance and the execution of initiatives, they will no longer tolerate black holes.

The future will also see black hole specialists and business process improvement specialists form a symbiotic relationship, one that greatly benefits customers.

AFTERWORD

This book places a great deal of attention on the human aspect of organizations. However, the writing of this book and the handling of black holes should not be considered "flakey", bleeding-heart exercises. Like mutating viruses, black holes have developed immense survival skills. They are pervasive and have persisted for a long time in organizations, despite the harm they cause. A hard-nosed, systematic approach, an understanding of organizations, and an iron will is required to eradicate black holes and terminate them for good. These skills are also needed to prevent black holes from draining the life and, if applicable, the profits out of every corner of today's organizations of size—including *Fortune* 500 and 1000 enterprises, medium-sized businesses, not-for-profit organizations, and government agencies. This broad claim can be difficult to accept, since government figures paint a rosy economic outlook and stock markets have risen to new highs. However, some experts believe that governments lie and publish false or misleading economic data to stay in power.[16] Other experts believe the United States Working Group on Financial Markets,[17, 18] also known as the "Plunge Protection Team," has been supporting and in fact driving up the DOW Jones Industrial Average and other indices for years, mainly for political reasons.[19] Plunge Protection Team or not, the vast quantity of liquidity[20] created out of nothing by the Federal Reserve and currently by the United States Treasury Department almost guarantees a rising DOW. That liquidity must go somewhere, until confidence in the fiat money experiment and the United States dollar collapses.

Gains can be made in the battle against black holes by reading this book, reviewing one's organization, and then taking appropriate action. However, such gains will be limited without the application of a structured approach to the discovery and the termination of the many deeply-rooted causes of black holes. Some of these causes are addressed in this book, but many can only be unearthed through formal analysis.

There is something new in the business landscape: a cutting-edge way to view organizations and improve their functionality. Many corporations that seem successful might question the need for improvement. However, if you feel you are constantly putting out fires and have no time to look for the source of the trouble, a black hole could be affecting your organization. If your company is not achieving its full potential, not returning full shareholder value, is fraught with personnel conflicts, or teetering on the brink of insolvency, a black hole could be draining your organization. Or your organization can *appear* fine yet still be the host of a black hole, because it takes time for black holes to manifest themselves on financial statements and elsewhere.

Trench work is never glorious, but this type of work was necessary to develop the technology to identify and eradicate black holes. Trench work is also required to fully implement the technology, because black holes must be eradicated in the board rooms *and particularly* in the "trenches".

The next wave of gains in organizational functionality will come from the bottom—where the majority of the human beings reside—not from the top.

About the Author

Ron entered the business world in his twenties assuming that management everywhere sought "organizational functionality." However, he would soon find out they did not.

A major component of organizational functionality, Ron thought, was the concept of repetitive actions by employees, and the smooth connectivity of these actions, as work, people, thoughts, documents, and materials flowed through the organization. He believed that the constant effort to improve efficiencies and the effectiveness of organizational functionality would not only be prized by top management, but also fought for feverishly in boardrooms and surrendered under no circumstances.

While working within organizations, Ron observed breakdowns in information flow, communications, and basic activities of company personnel. He asked himself, "This company has existed for decades, and it has developed complex manufacturing processes and logistics systems, so why is it failing to price an order correctly? Why is the ledger not balanced? Why are employees so frustrated? What is the quality of decision making at the top if its primary information is based on a consolidation of errors from the bottom?"

After witnessing breaks in the organizational functionality of several companies during his early years, Ron spent over five years in the highly process-oriented petrochemical industry. He again witnessed numerous breakdowns of organizational functionality, this time in a company whose greatest asset was its army of engineers. The petrochemical industry has deep pockets and some of the best minds in the world, nevertheless, Ron continued to witness a series of functional breaks and organizational failures. Ron's experiences in the "highly efficient" and "well run" petrochemical industry provided uncontested proof that something material was missing in the corporate world. The corporate universe did not align as it should. A black hole out there was absorbing the energy from organizational functionality.

Moving on from the petrochemical industry, and after taking a hiatus, Ron worked for the finance departments of a number of enterprises. He had the opportunity to look deep into the belly of organizations and see exactly what was, and was not, happening at all levels. He spent over five more years working relentlessly to understand organizational failure. Where had prior thinking gone wrong? What had executives and advisors missed? Why was there such a high degree of employee, and often customer, frustration? Why did so many organizations go through boom-and-bust cycles? Why were most business failures so quickly tossed into the "insufficient cash flow" bucket? Was it possible to correct the cause of draining cash flow? How could the company locate, handle, and terminate functional failings—for good?

Ron concluded that it was time to challenge conventional wisdom. From that conclusion a new technology was born. Relating to the part of the technology that spiders through organizations looking for functional disconnects, problems, and opportunities, Ron states, "It is not a perfect system; it is an intelligent system. It delivers the greatest degree of benefits for the least amount of cost and effort."

Ron asserts, "Black holes in organizations now have a tested and worthy adversary: Corporate Streamlining Technology—and black holes will collapse when they encounter the technology."

Ron Lutka, CMA, ACIS., P.ADM., CorpS, is the founder and president of Corporate Streamlining Company Inc., developer of Corporate Streamlining Technology, facilitator of the Corporate Streamlining Technology course, and a certified Corporate Streamliner. Ron was an avid ice hockey player in his youth, as a young adult he solo circumnavigated Lake Superior and Lake Huron in his twenty-five-foot sailboat, and he now resides in the Toronto, Canada, area with his girlfriend Liyu.

PART IV

REFERENCE MATERIAL

Appendix A

What Do Black Holes Look Like?

The intent of appendix A is to give the reader the opportunity to peer into a black hole. Various sections can be skipped, and the sections can be read in whatever order the reader wishes without loss of continuity. The appendix is lengthy because it is intended to be a helpful resource, one that you can put to immediate use to help determine if a black hole is harming your organization.

Real-life examples have been used where possible, with the names omitted and industries often changed. Some examples have been modified to make them more generally applicable.

In appendix A, I discuss what a black hole looks like from within. It is a fairly representative look into a typical black hole, although it is not comprehensive. Black hole-creating items are as plentiful as grains of sand in the Sahara Desert, so to list them all would be almost meaningless. Yet it is important for the reader to understand the types of items that can be either the causes or the by-products of black holes so the reader can *observe* and then determine if his organization is subject to a black hole and the damage such a black hole can cause. Please keep in mind that according to the definition of a black hole (found in chapter 1), there must be an *abundance* of undesirable activities or a *"lack of abundance"* of desirable activities, not merely an occasional occurrence. To clarify, the same few failures repeated many times can be classified as an "abundance" of undesirable activities.

Also, please keep in mind that black hole-creating items lead to much larger problems and opportunities than those presented in this appendix. For the most part, the emphasis in this appendix is on the *indicators* of a black hole rather than the *damage*. Damage perpetuated by black holes was discussed in chapters 1 through 4 and chapter 7.

Causes of Black Holes Transcend Departments

Often, improving organizational functionality is approached at the department level. Management consultants possess tomes on what to look for in the shipping department, another set of documents on what to look for in the treasury department, and yet another set of documents on what to look for in the production department. They often possess models of an ideal state for each department in an organization, or numeric targets that are usually based on industry norms.

These are valuable tools, but when it comes to identifying and dealing with black holes, these guidelines are incomplete. When a black hole is present in an organization, these guidelines can help flag a problem so people are aware it exists, but rarely do the guidelines themselves lead to the identification of causes. The causes of black holes in organizations are usually far more micro than traditional analysis is able to detect and, being micro, they transcend departments. They transcend departments because we are predominantly dealing with failures of basic building blocks common to all departments in all industries upon which larger problems sit.

Primarily because black hole-creating items transcend departments, this appendix has not been arranged by department as one might have expected.

Categories of Black Holes Overlap

When reading through the limited list in appendix A, you will likely notice a degree of overlap. This overlap exists because categories listed often have subcategories that are important enough to be categories on their own. Regardless, the categories that follow can be read independently, as each can stand on its own.

*   *   *

i)   A UPh Is Absent (Unifying Philosophy Statement)

Here is an example of overlapping categories: a UPh is a form of stable datum, yet section vi, "Data Is Unstable", has its own section. Since a UPh provides high-level direction that should be operationalized[21] throughout the organization, it overlaps with section xxvii, "The Ship Is Directionless."

What is a UPh? Allow Harish Chauhan, the creator of UPh, founder and president of Business by Philosophy to explain:

> A UPh is an 'all-in-one' strategic (built by the leadership), operational (managed and employed by all key stakeholders and staff), and market driven (designed for both customers and employees) statement constructed in 6 words or less. Succinctly and explicitly, a UPh captures a company's vision, values and raison d'être … thereby making it the company's 'DNA'. Over time and through company wide implementation, the UPh becomes the one corporate asset that is more practical and powerful than a logo, marketing tagline, or mission/vision statement. Benefits of a company UPh include stakeholder alignment, brand implementation, shareholder value maximization, culture and people development, exit strategy and business succession enhancement.

In my words, a UPh is that thin line of intention that runs through the founder of an organization and is transferred to the organization. It is the reason the founder created the company and is likely why the company continues to exist.

There are hundreds of shoe manufacturers, so why did Phil Knight and Bill Bowerman found Nike, Inc.? They each contributed five hundred dollars to establish Blue Ribbon Sports, which became Nike in 1972, a company that recorded $15 billion (USD) in revenues in its 2006 fiscal year and is reported to be the largest sports and fitness company in the world.[22, 23] Phil Knight and Bill Bowerman live that thin line of intention every day, and they instill a part of that intention, operationalizing it, in their employees and in Nike, Inc. In his first letter to shareholders as president and chief executive officer, Mark Parker might have given us a clue as to what that thin line of intention was when he wrote, "At the center of this success is the one thing that has driven Nike since day one—innovation."[24] A clue only, for innovation itself does not meet all the requirements of a UPh.

It is the thin line of intention that holds the power and the genius of the organization. When something this powerful and differentiating is lost, an organization wanders. Thoughts and actions within the organization begin to lose their alignment. And the organization takes its first baby steps to developing a black hole that can eventually cause it to act much like a water balloon. Have you ever held a balloon full of water in your hand? Try holding it so it retains its form. Difficult, isn't it?

Founders move on and even pass away. In some cases, the founder can no longer be relied upon to pull out of himself what that thin line of intention was that drove him to found the company. A well-thought-out UPh would lock in that intention.

Or perhaps the market shifted so much that the market the company was chasing is gone, and the company has forged on, creating new products for new markets and creating a new life for itself. That company exists in a marketplace, producing a product or service beside a number of other companies. If the company does not have a reason to exist different from that of its competitors, it might as well merge with its competitors, because there is no room for two identical companies in the marketplace. Two companies with similar philosophies create inefficiencies.

With that in mind, the first way to make an organization *black-hole-proof* (or to lessen the chances of a black hole forming) is to develop a UPh, then operationalize it throughout the company so that the UPh *is* the company. Every thought and action should then be aligned to support the UPh.

A success story of the UPh in practice demonstrates the effectiveness of this approach.

Example: A profitable food manufacturer named Breadsource Corporation was in search of a growth plan that would help it double its revenues in five years. Management, a family, was also in the midst of a critical business succession, from first to second generation. The ambitious sons wanted to take the company to new heights. Their immediate burdens were tight price margins, inconsistent customer pricing, extensive product waste, daily management crises, and poor-to-average employee morale. Even so, they persevered and developed a new company with a new brand identity and corporate strategy.

The UPh process assisted the stakeholders (the father and the two sons) in establishing core values and strategic guidelines, which became its *customer and corporate philosophy.* The thin line of intention, their UPh, is now expressed as "Freshness on Time."

With operational adjustments and testing to produce customer ordering, standardized pricing, new manufacturing and packaging benchmarks, and new distribution timelines, the "Freshness on Time" standard commanded, and realized, the following returns within five years of implementation:

1. The company doubled its revenues.

2. Roughly 70 percent of the company's customers came as a direct result of the UPh and its successful implementation.

3. Profit margins increased due to the guaranteed standard of freshness.

4. Waste rates of unused and unsold products decreased from a range of 4-6 percent to less than 1 percent, contributing significantly to profits.

5. Employee morale and training efficiency increased because the UPh was the only vision and the only day-to-day mission that had to be met within each employee's area of responsibility.

6. The company was successfully passed on to the second generation, bucking the typical rate of 60 percent of companies that fail when passed from the first to second generation.

7. Management now enjoys a more stable, streamlined, and strategic outlook on the company's daily operations and long-term future.

This is one of many scenarios in which companies that developed and consistently applied their UPh minimized, and often prevented, black holes within their organizations while establishing corporate prosperity and realizing extraordinary corporate performance and exceptional corporate well-being.

ii)   Dishonesty Is Present

"Dishonesty is present" is an obvious *What Do Black Holes Look Like?* item. The business landscape is littered with companies that rose to prominence based on lies, only to become names in the obituary column. Sometimes the lies carry forward for decades before an organization implodes and its executives are called on the carpet. Both off-balance-sheet liabilities and Enron Corporation come to mind.

Dishonesty creates enemies both inside and outside the organization, and enemies do not aid long-term survival and prosperity. Dishonesty harms sales and creates confusion in the workplace, hampering efficiencies and hurting production.

Dishonesty reduces reliability, whether reliability of the product or reliability of the liar. Dishonesty increases risk.

Example: It did not take long for bankruptcy to overcome a dishonest company that lied on its financial statements, underpaid suppliers (payments were based on a formula derived from sales), lied to the tax department, and lied to other government personnel and government agencies.

Ironically, the tactic of lying and the subsequent bankruptcy were both unnecessary. The company had the talent, the products, the contacts, and the capital to survive and prosper honestly. Sales were fine and growing. Margins were fair. Dishonesty saddled the company with severe and unnecessary complications, wasted talent and energy, and overwhelmed the business.

iii)   Backlogs Exist

Backlogs choke workflow because the backlogged station holds up stations downstream, which then experience costly idle time. When the backlog is resolved, the surge of work flowing downstream disrupts subsequent workstations, causing costly delays and possibly compromising quality as others down the chain take shortcuts to handle the surge. Borne out of backlogs, practices that compromise quality often become the new standard. And in a worst-case scenario, the new low standard might be terminal.

Whether the reasons for simple backlog situations are known or unknown, they can become life-threatening events for an already weak organization.

The issue of backlogs applies to both office work and plant work. If any of the following events are in play, then we have a situation that can cause black holes to form:

1. Management is unaware of the backlog situation.

2. Management is unaware that the backlog situation is causing resources downstream to sit idle.

3. Management is unaware that a method, or methods, used to relieve the backlog is lowering quality standards.

4. Management is unaware that relieving the backlog will create a surge downstream that can result in quality being compromised or might cause another backlog situation further downstream.

5. Management is unaware that a lower quality standard is about to become the new standard moving forward.

Issues in general are troublesome enough when management is aware of them, but they can be infinitely more troublesome if management is unaware of them.

Except in some situations where upcoming slack time will be sufficient to clear backlogs and still meet customer expectations, there is usually a cost to allowing backlogs to form. However, saving work to be processed in small batches to gain efficiencies or control is not considered backlogging for our purposes, unless it has a negative impact on the objectives of the organization, such as delaying shipments to customers.

In summary, backlogs choke organizations, waste resources, cause idleness and surges, and compromise quality. Quality compromises might be short term, but such compromises can also result in quality being reduced to a new lower standard moving forward.

Example 1:   A manufacturer purchased a high volume of prefabricated drawers from one supplier on an ongoing basis. The supplier was a small company and the manufacturer was their largest customer, so the supplier did not want to create hostilities and, therefore, did not create much of an issue about the manufacturer being far behind on paying invoices.

When the manufacturer fell one million dollars behind in payments, the supplier began experiencing cash flow problems. The supplier raised his concerns with the manufacturer's controller and its chief financial officer. The controller looked into the supplier's account and agreed that the manufacturer was behind on payments. However, the amount, according to the manufacturer, was less than one hundred thousand dollars, which the company paid to bring the account current.

The supplier grew severely stressed and threatened to stop the delivery of drawers if the large liability was not addressed. The controller and the chief financial officer looked into the supplier's account again and saw it was fairly current. The supplier's threats eventually prompted the chief financial officer to hire an outside firm to look into the accounts payable process.

After a review, it was found that a clerk was four months behind in entering this supplier's invoices into the accounts payable sub-ledger. When the backlog was handled, the official amount owing the supplier skyrocketed. The manufacturer issued the supplier a large check, and a potential manufacturing stoppage was avoided.

Example 2:   An international manufacturer in the transportation industry was backlogged in the corporate secretary function. The many banks this organization dealt with in several countries forgave them for failing to send key banking documents and corporate resolutions that had not yet been drafted or passed; however, the risk of a bank not honouring checks increased with each month the company lagged behind in its filings.

The company was also far behind in its statutory government filings. The company no longer had a stand-alone corporate secretary, so the vice president of finance added that duty to his many responsibilities. In addition to being the chief financial officer, he became the corporate secretary. However, he was already bogged down running the finance side of a fast-moving international company and had little time to resolve the backlog relating to the corporate secretary function.

Outside help was brought in to work with the company's officers and directors, as well as the officers and directors of all of its subsidiaries, and to work with outside lawyers in each country to bring all filings, bank documents, and corporate resolutions to current status. Handling the backlog reduced the chance of check-clearing being delayed, smoothed relations at the banks, and eased the minds of the company's officers and directors, as this was fast becoming a significant internal and external compliance issue.

iv)   Disconnects Have Formed

The definition of "disconnect" in the corporate streamlining sense is a permanently broken, or intermittently broken, flow that should be flowing routinely, including *poor or omitted handoffs*. It could mean a broken written or oral communication flow, a broken material flow, a broken product flow, a broken flow of bodies (as in a "no-show" situation), or even a broken flow of thoughts or ideas.

Example 1:   A financial controller instructed an invoicing clerk to issue customers credit notes for goods returned in good order, as determined by the shipper/receiver. The invoicing clerk did not understand the instructions (and the controller did not ensure the instructions were understood). Without receiving credit notes due, the customers refused to pay unpaid invoices and so cash flow becomes impaired—all due to a breakdown in communication flow.

Example 2: Raw materials, consumable supplies, or component parts did not arrive at the workstations by the time they were needed. This was a breakdown in material flow.

Example 3: There were gaps in product flows to regional distribution centers, which left the distributors short of product and long on customer complaints. This was a breakdown in product flow.

Example 4: A meeting was called by the vice president of production to determine the cause of deteriorating quality. Not present at the meeting was a machine operator with nine years' service, whom the vice president of production did not like and so did not invite. The machine operator was aware that the plant's quality reporting system had been abandoned by plant personnel over time and routine adjustments to root causes of poor quality were no longer being made. Since this awareness never reached the vice president of production, the resolution of the poor quality issue was delayed. This was a breakdown in thought or ideas flow.

Example 5: The annual budget for a metal stamping plant was not communicated to the machine operators on the plant floor. Historically, the budget was relayed by way of established machine run-speed standards; however, this method was discontinued. Therefore, synchronization of machine run-speeds to the annual budget could not be monitored by management. Production was unable to match budget expectations, despite the plant operating twenty-four hours per day, seven days per week, less maintenance downtime. This was a breakdown in communication flow.

Example 6: The storehouse for all necessary parts and consumables was located at one end of a long plant. The packing and shipping function used a high volume of materials. Personnel wasted time either walking the length of the plant to pick up frequently needed material or waiting for a tow-motor to deliver material. A storage area for high-volume packing and shipping material near the packing and shipping area would have resolved this breakdown in material flow.

Example 7:   The enthusiastic marketing department of a heating, ventilation, and air conditioning company launched a huge springtime campaign that created demand far in excess of the company's ability to deliver and install central air conditioners. This was not only a breakdown in product flow, but also in communication flow, since the marketing department did not ask the installation department about its capacity to meet increased product demand.

Example 8:   Equipment installations were behind schedule because not enough mechanics were available to travel to customer job sites. This was a breakdown in body flow.

Example 9:   A pricing manager had the answer to faster month-end closings, but because of his animosity toward the director of finance, he withheld the information. This was a breakdown in the flow of ideas.

v)   **Inconsistencies Impede Actions**

Inconsistencies within an organization can take many forms, such as the ones listed below:

1. Management reports conflict, whether written or verbal.
2. Two terms have the same meaning.
3. The same term is given two meanings.
4. Action is inconsistent with goals, plans, or policies.
5. Product colour, dimensions, or packaging varies when not desired.
6. Delivery times vary dramatically when not desired.
7. Management communicates inconsistent messages in policy documents, speeches, programs, employee reprimands, awards, directives, annual budgets, and so on.
8. Company's abilities do not align with market's wants and needs.

Example 1:   The new president of an industrial material manufacturer wanted to know the plant output for the previous month. The vice president of operations, the controller, and the shipper each gave him a different answer.

It is not that we are inconsistent, Mr. Pigsley. It is just that we give you different answers to the same questions.

Example 2:   Confusion during senior management meetings frequently arose because managers were confusing the terms "budget" and "plan." Someone familiar with the company's budget observed the chaos and frustration and noticed this inconsistency. He advised the management team to adopt definitions that reflected his observations:

Budget: The annual budget; a specific type of plan with dollar and production input and output figures built into it. The annual budget does not change, once adopted.

Plan: An intention to do something. Within this organization, the written plan started out as the budget; however, whereas the annual budget figures are fixed for the year, the plan figures are revised monthly, as needed.

Once the inconsistency in word use was corrected, managers understood one another and the meetings became calmer and more productive.

Example 3:   A manufacturing company had a policy of installing water filtration systems within twenty-four hours of the installation department receiving the work orders and materials. Every morning, the service and installation department issued work orders to installers, who would pick up their materials from the holding area and then set out to install the water filtration systems. Often the installers did not finish all the work orders they had received in the morning. Since the company did not have a tracking system to record work orders from issuing through to completion, the installers decided when to complete which work orders, resulting in some water filtration systems not being installed for weeks because installers completed the easy installations first and left the difficult ones for slow work periods. Actions were inconsistent with policies.

Example 4:   Nortel's abilities do not always align with the market's wants and needs.

This is a difficult thing for Nortel to manage, because the market they cater to booms and busts and shifts right and left and up and down. Nortel cannot realign itself as fast as the market moves, despite many good intentions to do so. Plants cannot scale up and scale down quickly. Talent cannot be hired and properly trained or laid off efficiently. Capital cannot be raised and retired at every market turn. Products cannot be developed and tested, and plans cannot be drawn and launched to keep in sync with every market hiccup—and so Nortel's return on capital suffers at times.

vi)   Data Is Unstable

The definitions of "syntropy" and "entropy" were given in chapter 2, "What Causes the Formation of Black Holes?"

Stable data can help management and employees leverage their syntropic ability by implementing tools that foster ability and organization and reduce the chance of error. Manuals, policies and procedures, reconciliation, standardization, and checklists are a few well-known stabilizing tools. We discuss standardization separately below.

One big contributor to the formation of black holes in organizations is the failure to transfer the knowledge or guidelines contained in the stabilizing documentation to the users of the information. Would you let a pilot who has never read a pilot's manual fly your plane? If not, why would you allow front-line troops and supervisors who have not read the policy and procedures manuals, or who do not fully understand their content, to operate a company?

There are millions of people employed right now who have never read their desk manual, department policies and procedures manual, safety manual, quality-control manual, equipment manual, or other guidelines or instructions pertinent to their position. I do not mean they should read it through one time, although that would be a great improvement. I mean they should read it, re-read it, and understand it so they—clerks, supervisors, and managers—can quote sections from these stabilizing documents as easily as they can rattle off baseball and hockey pool statistics.

I believe the content of stabilizing documents is important to the smooth functioning of organizations. It is important that employees *know* what is in those documents. If you agree with me and you want your employees to be able to apply the information contained in those documents, create a quiet room and initially require employees to spend four or five hours per week studying the materials. Yes! Let's get serious about our organizations! Taper that off to some lower number permanently, and then watch your organization take shape—and calm down.

Putting plenty of attention on stabilizing documents will help the organization function the way management designed. Employees will also be better positioned to find new and improved ways for the organization to operate as they compare their in-the-trenches experiences to the designed way of operating. Perpetually updating the documents to reflect management's intentions and better ways of operating is valuable, and will become easy if given enough attention.

Organizations with black holes tend to have stabilizing documents that are deficient or improperly put into practice. Here, we see a significant disconnect. Management develops policies and procedures, or commissions someone to develop them. Then, management adopts them but goes no further than producing thick books that too often get buried. It is fascinating to slog through the belly of a troubled organization and review the policies and procedures manuals and witness the disconnection.

A management that does not view policies and procedures as live documents will resist change, and resisting change will lead to disuse of policies and procedures and the formation of a black hole. If the policies and procedures are not doable, or are doable but do not make good business sense, it is management's problem, and the "doers" should notify management. If policies and procedures do make sense, then it is operation's problem, so operations needs to follow them.

Update the documents based on newly discovered opportunities, and then pass this knowledge on to employees by requiring them to study the new material. In this way, over time, your organization will ratchet itself up. People will become part of a more efficient, more effective, and better-functioning organization.

The following extract from Business Process Trends' "The State of Business Process Management: 2006" survey clearly shows there is ample room to tighten documentation within organizations:

Are Work Processes Documented?

We actually asked if work processes were documented and kept up to date. Any organization that undertakes a process redesign or an ISO certification effort creates some kind of process documentation. Only companies with a real commitment to processes have a system that consistently maintains process documentation. We weren't surprised that those who bothered to take this survey had some documentation; we weren't surprised that almost half only Occasionally had up to date documentation. We were pleasantly surprised that almost a quarter of our respondents said that their organizations Frequently had their process documentation up to date and that another quarter had up to date documentation Most of the Time. (See Figure 9.)

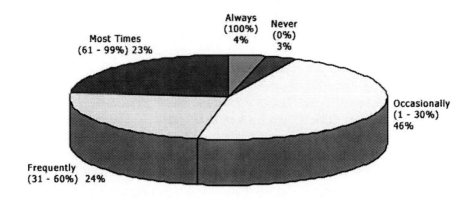

Work processes are documented and documentation is kept up to date

Reproduced by permission *from The State of Business Process Management, 2006, fig. 9* [25]

Large companies are a little more likely to respond to this question by saying Frequently, and midsized companies are slightly more likely to respond Occasionally. North American companies are slightly more likely to say Occasionally than companies from other countries that are more likely to distribute their responses as displayed above.

vii)   Opportunities for Standardization Are Missed

Standardization is another tremendous organization stabilizer. "Standardization" equals "routine" equals "more familiarity, faster handling, and fewer errors."

Everyone is familiar with standardization on the plant floor. The plant floor exudes it: fill the five-pound bags of flour with five pounds of flour; make the foot-long hot dogs one foot long; put a minimum of fifteen grams of protein in every protein bar that leaves the plant; manufacture OFF! Deep Woods to include 23.8 percent DEET; manufacture Listerine with 0.091 percent eucalyptol; ship using twenty-foot and forty-foot shipping containers; use forty-eight-inch skids.

The benefits of standardization are clear: customers know what they are getting, craftsmen know what they are doing, and frontline workers know what is expected of them. When employees must repeat an action, they should find it known and predictable. Having done it successfully today, workers are confident in their ability to do it tomorrow. In the freeze-drying process, deep-frozen products are dried at temperatures below -18°C (0°F). This is the freeze-drying process operator's standard, and it stabilizes his actions. Each day he arrives at work, he does not need to guess through trial and error what temperature he should use to freeze-dry food. This action is standardized. The worker only needs to *execute* each day, not *determine*.

Two common actions that are rarely standardized, but often should be, are *requests for assistance* and *directives issued*. They should be standardized, especially in hectic environments, because so often requests for assistance and directives issued are not subsequently executed by the receiving party. Managers quit in frustration because they are not able to gain control over the people in their area. Requests for assistance, formalized on paper or electronically, put the request into the physical world, where it becomes far more real and controllable. Work becomes less of a fuzzy, nebulous experience and more concrete. The chances of a black hole forming are reduced.

Standardization improves data collection, reduces error in data transfer and in execution, dramatically speeds up data handling time and activity execution time, makes it easier to catch errors, makes it easier to correct errors, makes work flow more smoothly and predictably, reduces supervision time, reduces training time, can foster transparency by way of reports and statistics, and makes the workplace a much more stable and pleasant environment.

Example: There are plenty of opportunities for standardization within an office environment. Here are some examples:

1. Sales orders
2. Quality deviation forms
3. Branch cash flow statements
4. Branch profit and loss statements
5. Computer hardware and software used by all branches
6. Cash application forms
7. Purchase requisitions

8. Purchase orders
9. Sales contracts
10. Distribution agreements
11. Locations to drop completed work
12. Expense reports
13. Requests for price overrides and subsequent approval
14. Various other approval documents
15. Requests for assistance or directives (work orders).

viii)   Business Controls Are Lacking

The topic of business controls, with the exception of black holes, is thoroughly covered in many textbooks and reference materials issued by most accounting bodies, therefore I will only lightly cover this area.

"Business controls are lacking" sits near section vi, "Data Is Unstable", because a lack of controls allows organizations to destabilize. Conversely, controls help stabilize organizations.

An organization that allows a serious black hole to form most likely has a lack-of-controls issue, because controls would help flag the damage early so it could then be addressed, at least to some degree. However, controls cost money and require discipline. The person responsible for implementing and enforcing controls must understand the benefits to be derived from them. That is not always the case in an organization with a black hole.

There are plenty of areas where controls can help reduce the formation of black holes. Implementing controls to maintain data integrity downstream and not letting bad data into the organization in the first place will both go a long way toward ironing out some problems.

The controls that can be implemented in an organization are almost endless; the starting point to implementing controls is not. The starting point to implementing controls is an *intention*. The actualization of that intention brings about control. A director does not want to be personally sued, so he puts controls in place to ensure that the organization is constantly in full compliance with various standards, such as environmental laws and regulations. He also asks the company to purchase directors' and officers' liability insurance.

A chief financial officer wants to contain costs, so she implements a guide containing spending approval limits. The vice-president of marketing has the intention of increasing contribution margins, so he asks accounting to align data so he knows what his contribution margins are, based on each product sold. The vice president of operations wants to ensure that raw materials are available for use tomorrow, so she constructs a fence around the material in the yard today.

"Intention" always precedes "business controls." It might be argued that black holes are the absence of intention, but they are the absence of attention as well.

Example: A custom manufacturer in the geotextile industry, producing twenty-four hours per day, seven days per week—except for scheduled and unscheduled downtime—produced a certain amount of product year-to-date which fell far below budgeted expectations.

No attempt was made to account for the budget shortfall in production. It was observed but not analyzed. Since the plant was operating continuously, the budget shortfall was a screaming failure, because resources were being used to the maximum, which meant that the budget could not be met. The issue needed attention but received none, until one person, not in the chain of command, took it upon himself to look into the matter. When he did, he found the machine outputs assumed in the budget to be far in excess of what the machines could produce. He also found the start-up times and change-over times (machine down time) defined in the budget to be far less than those actually incurred. This was vital data. Knowing this, one could then look for root causes as to why *actual* varied from *budget*, with the intention of aligning the two. Since one of the executive team's greatest control tools is the annual budget, retooling machinery or re-engineering the budget was required so that the next budget would be meaningful.

ix) Spirits Are "Broken"

There are benefits to viewing people as "spirits" and organizations as "organisms." I believe management would benefit by viewing organizations as organisms that use mechanical tools, rather than viewing the organization itself as a mechanical tool. Organizations obtain stellar results when they approach people and organizations this way.

If people are spirits, and if spirits can be "broken," then it is important that the people who pay the bills know this, if they want the people they pay to be creative and productive.

A spirit can break when a clerk is threatened by a superior for notifying employees of a significant safety hazard the superior wanted to keep buried. And a spirit can break by experiencing a series of hits that compound over time, such as when an employee is constantly blamed for problems he did not create. In both cases, decreased performance usually follows. Multiply circumstances such as these across time and across the population of sections, departments, divisions, or an entire organization, and you can see why willingness to help, productivity, creativity, and problem-solving can suffer dramatically.

The most common causes of "broken" spirits in organizations, in my experience, have been *fear, apathy,* and *anger*. One of the tactics used by people who suppress employees is to create fear. Both the carrot and the stick have motivating aspects, but fear is a double-edged sword. What one gains in compliance, one loses in creativity, problem solving, productivity, communication, and functionality as employees clam up and pull back. If an employee, or anyone for that matter, is suppressed often enough over a long enough period, that person can become apathetic and almost lifeless. Try getting productivity out of a lifeless person!

Firmness, when appropriate, is very different from suppression. The difference can be found by understanding *justice* versus *injustice*. Firmness, when appropriate, is constructive and just; suppression never is.

I am sure Mother Nature did not expect her highest life form would have to protect themselves from each other.

Anger can also be a manifestation of a "broken" spirit, depending on why one is angry. Anger rooted in injustice is certainly a manifestation of a "broken" spirit.

Apathy, fear, anger. These are not states you want people in your organization to manifest. People have complex lives and assorted problems that can cause them to feel a certain way, but when most people in an organization, or in one area of an organization, feel apathetic, fearful, or angry, the source most likely can be found within the organization.

The following are examples of how fear, apathy, and anger can manifest in organizations:

Example 1:   A manufacturing division of a company had major problems. Shipments were late, goods were being shipped incomplete, installations were behind schedule, and the company was losing money. Many employees had insight into how to resolve the problems plaguing the organization; however, the person in charge of the division wielded a great deal of power within the organization. He was the biggest problem, despite being very valuable in other ways. The employees knew this, but head office did not. This manager's style struck fear into the employees daily. The bottom line was that all the problems persisted and the employees did not offer solutions until this manager left the organization.

Example 2:   A whole section of stockbrokers was beaten to the ground because they were unsuccessful at selling in-house underwritings of stock offerings. Instead of management rooting out the causes of the inability to sell, namely, deals heavily biased in favour of the company rather than the customers, it shirked its duties. Apathy screams out at you when you see it.

Example 3:   A highly talented manager led teams of outside contractors and inside employees that performed troubleshooting and resolved significant problem areas of a company. Over the years, the manager was asked to handle several hot trouble spots.

This man drove the teams hard, yet methodically, to meet his and the company's objectives. The team succeeded and the manager has many letters of praise from top executives to prove it. A new senior executive joined the company and became the troubleshooter's boss. From that point forward, all the troubleshooter's accomplishments were claimed by the new boss. The new boss would tell other senior executives what "he" had found and what "he" had done to fix the problems. He would do this by phone and e-mail, and also during formal presentations while the troubleshooter was present. The troubleshooter was angry. His accomplishments were more valuable than his paychecks, and the new executive was robbing him blind. This stellar troubleshooter left the now hostile environment and the organization lost a proven performer.

x)   Root Causes Are Ignored

Within black holes, root causes of problems are rarely tracked down and resolved. There might be several reasons for this. Perhaps the staff is so mired in day-to-day complexities that they do not have the time required to find the root cause of recurring problems. Staff might lack the ability to find the root cause or might be discouraged from doing so, based on previous experiences in which management took no action to terminate root causes that they identified. Staff might be discouraged from tracking down root causes because they are being suppressed by someone who does not want the truth exposed. Failing to track down and terminate the root cause of recurring problems is a high-level, black hole-creating item.

Example 1:   The inventory level of an electronics distributor would periodically balloon. The controller would then panic and call in several managers, supervisors, and warehouse workers, and the group would brainstorm ways to reduce the inventory. Customers were offered discounts, inventory was sold to liquidators, and the company pleaded with suppliers to take back stock for partial credits. This cycle repeated every so often, until someone studied the situation with a root-cause approach. The distributor was receiving massive returns from customers but still ordering more product because returns were not being scanned into the management-information system on a timely basis. A review of inventory in the warehouse revealed twenty-two skids of product that one customer had returned over four months earlier and which had not been entered into the system. The staff responsible for managing stock purchases did not know the product was available for shipment to other customers.

These discoveries led to management action, which led to improved inventory management.

Example 2:   There were constant price differences between the amount due on invoices and the amount the customer was willing to pay. The sales department was frequently pulled in to help settle matters and would usually approve the amount the customer said was due. This went on for months, until an individual tracked down the root cause of the problem. He discovered that the pricing department was using an outdated contract. Pricing had not received the new contracts which both parties had signed six months earlier. To solve the problem, the company created a pricing distribution checklist and attached it to the front of all new contracts. This simple process ensured that those who needed contracts received them.

Example 3:   The senior management of a national distribution company was preparing the annual budget. Management was having difficulty accepting the fact that its budgeted gross margins based on prior years' actual data were far below the target. In fact, the budgeted gross margins were almost non-existent. Management crunched the numbers every which way, but the bottom line remained unacceptable. The problem occurred because the multitude of sales incentives and side deals that chewed margins down had never been previously disclosed in the annual budget and so were never addressed. Once disclosed, the business model had to change if management wanted margins to improve. However, this did not occur and the company soon filed for bankruptcy.

xi) Data Integrity Is Poor

For the most part, black hole-creating data-integrity issues break down as follows:

1. During a computer software conversion, data carried over from a previous system is indiscernible or difficult to recognize in the new system.

Example: All outstanding payments made against accounts payables (i.e., "on account" payments that were not used to clear invoices payable) were rolled into one lump-sum per supplier account in the new system. When a project team looked into finding supporting documents for these payments, the trail led them to the previous software system. The project team had to locate an old computer terminal and learn how to use the old system, including discovering what the previous passwords were. Once they could operate the old system, they used the data to identify check numbers and dates and then located cancelled checks, which could then be presented to suppliers to help reconcile the accounts.

We could add "loss of knowledge on how to access information in old computer system" as a black hole-creating data integrity issue.

2. Missing source documents

Example: A company's balance sheet included various tax payable and tax receivable balances that could not be supported by source documents.

3. Human error in data entry or raw data interpretation during manual data recording

Example: When looking at a drawing e-mailed from a branch, the data entry clerk misinterpreted a nine for a seven. The cabinet was manufactured two feet too narrow. The previous day, data entry entered code 22 (walnut stain with Varathane finish) instead of correctly entering code 2 (white satin finish), resulting in the wrong finish being applied to the cabinet.

4. Covert and malicious human activity, ranging from nuisance to sabotage

Example: Employees who are paid by the competition to ruin an organization, criminals, disgruntled employees, and incompetents can and do destroy the integrity of data. This malicious activity is broad ranging—falsifying a receiving document, altering the calculations within the organization's pricing model, issuing false statements stating tons of silver backs certificates when in fact no silver backs the certificates, etc.

5. Failure to implement basic edit checks and perform reconciliation

Example: Knowing that humans make errors, as noted in point 3 above, businesses would be wise to focus on reducing the number of mistakes. Edit checks are an easy and inexpensive way to catch errors, and then correct them, before they contaminate the system. At one organization, branch codes consisted of three characters. An edit check was put in place using a look-up table that contained all the branch codes. If a code was entered that did not match a code in the table, an automated warning was issued.

6. Software miscalculations arising from faulty programming

Example: Software miscalculations can result in data-integrity issues both minor and significant—for example, volume rebate calculations that have an incorrect payment formula. For instance, a program that calculates volume rebates at 5 percent of a value, when the volume rebate calculation should be 0.5 percent, would result in poor data integrity.

7. Corrupted data within the database (source can be electrical, viral, or user- or software-related)

Example: A construction company's software program would corrupt and then reject certain cash application entries, tossing them into a "failed entry" list. The IT department was aware of the problem, and one IT staff person reallocated rejected entries to their correct accounts weekly; however, data integrity was still impaired prior to the entries being reallocated weekly.

8. Poor administration of contracts

Example: Poor administration of contracts is a data-integrity issue because the records do not properly reflect what is owing to the organization. Conversely, liabilities might not be properly reflected in the organization's records. Since "data integrity" means the data represents what it states, we have data-integrity failure. At an oil company, contracts with restaurants across Canada specified lease terms. The organization's data integrity was poor because the restaurants owed over $100,000 in back rent that was not recorded on the organization's books. This data-integrity issue was rectified with a few letters and phone calls to the restaurants, followed by the collection of the back rent, check deposits, and then journal entries that were applied to the organization's books. Once this was accomplished, the organization's data correctly reflected the current status of the lease agreements with the restaurants.

9. Poor data-capture processes and procedures that fail to capture important data or fail to capture the data in a usable form

Example: The marketing department of a large national distributor actively cut co-op advertising deals with large retail customers, but neglected to notify the invoicing department. As a result, valid customer credits were not issued to customers. In this case, the poor data integrity caused an off-book liability to grow to over $1 million. The amount was subsequently written off the organization's books to restore data integrity.

10. Too few categories into which data can be entered or consolidated, or category choices that misrepresent the data

Example: Evidence suggests the International Monetary Fund might have countenanced the practice of central banks throwing gold loans receivable (including gold swaps) into the same balance sheet account as gold bullion, even though this violates well-known and standardized Generally Accepted Accounting Principles (GAAP). A receivable has counter-party risk attached to it, whereas fully paid-for gold is nobody's liability. Lumping the two distinctly different asset classes—the loans receivable and the less risky gold account—together in one account on the balance sheet severely compromises data integrity. Gold investors, hard-money advocates, and many concerned citizens of certain nations are up in arms about this apparent contrivance, because if true, it hides the size of gold loans (including swaps) issued by central banks, hides the amount of gold sold into the marketplace, hides the dwindled central bank gold bullion holdings, and puts national treasury gold bullion loaned to undisclosed counter-parties at risk.[26, 27]

11. Failure to use a management-information system as designed

Example: A large woodworking manufacturer processed a high volume of orders every month and had a system for tracking these orders from the moment the order was accepted by the company to the time it was delivered to  the customer—and beyond, since the records were retained for many years. This organization was definitely experiencing the effects of a black hole, because thousands of orders that were completed long ago remained in the management information system as "work in progress," and so reports drawn off the system were unusable.

12. Laziness

   Example: If people do not do simple things, like adding check totals to
               worksheets, reviewing their work for reasonableness, and follow-
               ing up to ensure that what was intended to occur did occur,
               then data will deteriorate. A payroll supervisor never checked
               the bank statements to ensure her payroll checks had cleared
               correctly, and she never gave the person who reconciled the
               bank accounts a list of the specific amounts that should have
               cleared. Last we heard, the bank account did not reconcile, and
               the payroll amounts that had cleared the bank did not total the
               amounts on the payroll records.

xii)   Management Reports Are Created from Inaccurate Data

Please refer to the triangle below, with hundreds of specks dotting the lower two-
thirds and bricks composing the top third. This illustration demonstrates that the
bricks at the top, which represent management reports, can be no more truthful than
the source data represented by the hundreds of specks covering the bottom two-
thirds. In fact, they are often much less truthful, because data that does not conve-
niently fit into management-requested pigeonholes is often arbitrarily dumped into
other pigeonholes. Therefore, the higher up the reporting-consolidation ladder one
goes, the greater the watering down or deterioration of data one finds.

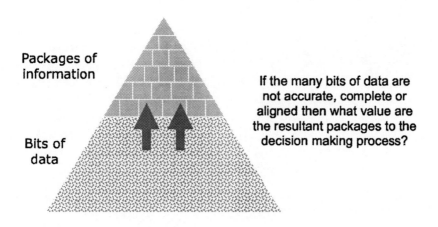

Packages of
information

Bits of
data

If the many bits of data are
not accurate, complete or
aligned then what value are
the resultant packages to the
decision making process?

In addition, the source data, for many of the reasons we have outlined, may be
suspect. Please think about this for a moment. The data consolidated into man-

agement reports can be no better than the source data, meaning management reports can have no more integrity than that of the data used to create the reports. Resolving the issue of data integrity is a prerequisite to sound management reporting.

Example 1:   Distributors frequently phoned the president of a manufacturer asking for commission money due to them. The president would ask finance for commission statements and then would argue with the distributors about the amounts owing to them. The distributors would invariably supply supporting documents to back up their claims. The president would pass these documents on to finance, and finance staff would then scramble to investigate the distributors' claims—only to find that in almost every case, the distributors were correct. The problem? The manufacturer's system for tracking distributors' commissions was woefully inadequate. This was a data-integrity issue that a well-thought-out management-reporting system could have identified earlier.

Example 2:   A very busy heavy-industry manufacturer experienced many equipment breakdowns and long delays when restarting machines. The manufacturer kept an unusually large number of spare parts, over four thousand *different* parts, in the store-house—or so they thought, according to the management reports. However, the reports were not accurate. In reality, 25 percent of the spare part bins were empty, forcing machine operators and maintenance crews to issue purchase requisitions for required parts, then wait days for the parts to arrive. This too was a data-integrity issue that a well-thought-out management-reporting system could have identified earlier.

xiii)   Potential "Time Bombs" Are Hidden

Potential "time bombs" hidden within organizations are a fascinating area of study. Our definition of a potential hidden "time bomb" is:

the existence within an organization of a potential event, not readily visible, that can cause significant damage to the long-term survival or prosperity of the organization should it occur.

Next in importance are *potential known "time bombs"*. Here are three examples of the many potential "time bombs" we have identified in organizations:

Example 1: An organization was suffering from marked deterioration in the quality of products produced and shipped. Management refused to accept that quality was deteriorating, therefore it took no action to address the potential of losing sales and customers. Kabang! The potential event became a real event, as major customers refused shipments and eventually customers were lost.

Example 2: An organization operating with over one hundred distributorships, many of them unhappy, had few distributorship agreements signed and in force. This left the organization open to a potentially harmful event: many or all of the  distributors moving to a different supplier. Last we heard, no kabang. But the potential of one still exists.

Example 3: A distributor did not have a good system for tracking returns from customers, then subsequently returning them to their manufacturing suppliers within the allotted time to receive a credit. Therefore, a potential harmful event (missing the "return to supplier for credit" window) existed each time a customer returned a product. Kabang! Millions of dollars of obsolete inventory accumulated, unknown to management, then were written off because suppliers refused to accept huge volumes of returns presented to them after their deadlines.

Here are two examples of potential *financial* "time bombs":

Example 1: Long Term Capital Management was founded by Nobel Prize laureates. Despite being the creation of geniuses, LTCM failed in 1998 when the market moved against a derivative position with a notional principal amount in excess of $1 trillion that was backed by merely $4 billion in capital.[28] Actual events, way out on the tails of the probability distribution curve, had kicked in. The highly *improbable* but distinctly *possible* occurred. That is the essence of potential "time bombs" in organizations.

Example 2:   LTCM was then; this is now. What potential hidden financial "time bombs" lurk today? Strangely, despite the world's experience with LTCM, there are still many potential hidden "time bombs"—interest rates, foreign exchange, oil, gold, and silver derivatives, especially in the unregulated over-the-counter market. Derivatives in the over-the-counter market totaling US$370 trillion (yes, trillion) are outstanding as of June 30, 2006 (up from $281 trillion on June 30, 2005), according to the Bank for International Settlements.[29] Add to that another $84 trillion in exchange-traded derivatives.[30] These derivatives are a potential hidden "time bomb" because (1) derivatives are a massive and extremely highly leveraged affair, mostly conducted in the unregulated over-the-counter market; (2) derivatives place great power in the hands of parties likely to abuse that power; and (3) derivatives entail counter-party risk.

Potential hidden "time bombs" and potential "time bombs" are a fascinating study for at least three reasons:

1. One unaddressed or insufficiently addressed potential "time bomb" can develop into a mammoth, destructive fireworks display that can sink an organization by itself.
2. Management complacency about the existence and nature of potential "time bombs" remains a puzzle.
3. At the core of a potential "time bomb," one might find the fingerprints of a spirit gone bad—a criminal.

xiv)   Key Data Is Insufficiently Balanced

This is actually a data-integrity issue, but we have pulled it out as a separate item to highlight its importance.

Attempts to balance key data are often insufficient and fail because the integrity of the data at the lower levels is poor—likely for one or some of the reasons listed under section xi, "Data Integrity Is Poor." Rather than trying to close the barn doors—spending hours trying to balance the high level data—after the horse has left the barn, management resigns itself to plugging differences with arbitrary data to make reports balance.

"Comparing dissimilar data" is another reason, and an acceptable one, as long as the user of the data is aware dissimilar data is being compared. Too often, that is not the case.

If management wants to decrease risk and the amount of time spent trying to reconcile differences between reports and decrease the degree of executive frustration caused by trying to understand reports, it will attempt to tighten data integrity at the lower levels.

Example 1: A national lighting distributor was selling lighting units to major retail accounts across the country. Although the distributor was shipping the lighting units, it was not invoicing customers for all units. A comparison between shipments for each month and the total number of units invoiced for each month would have helped management flag this issue.

Example 2: A manufacturer of fireplaces issued invoices for each fireplace it shipped, but it did not balance fireplaces produced versus fireplaces shipped. If the manufacturer had done so, it would have caught the criminal ring producing and selling fireplaces for its own profit a lot sooner.

xv) Productivity Is Insufficiently Measured

Measurement of plant personnel productivity in aggregate rather than on a more micro basis—preferably per individual—leads to black holes forming in organizations. And so does insufficient measurement of office personnel productivity.

Organizations often have some measure of plant personnel productivity but little or no measure of office personnel productivity. "I have no idea what these people do," a vice president of sales and marketing admitted to me in frustration one day. He was referring to the office clerks in *his* sales and marketing department!

Why shouldn't the productivity of office personnel be measured? It might be difficult to measure the weekly productivity of the controller, but it is not difficult to measure the productivity of individual pricing personnel, accounts payable staff, quality control employees, schedulers, or the payroll clerk. I agree that some office personnel handle only what hits their desk, such as invoices from customers, and they are not productive unless work is flowing to them (which is another reason to avoid bottlenecks in the system). Their productivity can be measured, however, and with productivity data in hand, supervisors and managers can see who the star clerks are and who the laggards are. They can discover the capacity of a department and what slack, if any, exists in the system. As these unknowns become known, managers can begin to tighten up their ship.

Not knowing productivity numbers of office personnel who perform repetitive tasks is like not knowing how far your car will go (production) on a tank of gas (employee). The result, expressed as a rate, is "productivity." This is a potential black hole-creating item, because each function within the organization is competing for scarce capital. If one section is wasting capital, another section might be deprived of the funds to repair other black hole-creating items. Do you see how subtle black holes can be? Do you also see the damage black holes can cause, even if they expand at a glacial pace—slowly yet relentlessly—until they have gouged a hole in the organization as huge as the Great Lakes?

Where is your productivity data?

Example: Management did not know what an invoicing clerk's productivity numbers were. This allowed the invoicing clerk to complain of overload and convince management that she needed part-time help. A review of the area revealed that it was not an issue of volume but rather of organization (or lack thereof), due to poor workflow between departments. This organization needed a better way to arrange the sequence of invoice printing, and a dedicated printer, as well as a new, more certain, and more timely flow of invoice attachments. Once organization and workflow changes were made, the invoice clerk handled the work well alone—and she now enjoys her work.

xvi)   Blame Replaces Problem Solving

When an organization deteriorates substantially, there will come a point where destructive blame replaces constructive problem solving.

People who manage organizations must ensure that employees are competent and remove them when they are not, but when we talk about "blame" replacing "problem solving," we are talking about a systemic problem, not a problem of employee incompetence. Misdirected blame is largely a function of the growing inability of the organization to resolve problems for a variety of reasons, usually related to black holes.

Those reasons can include a sudden, unforeseeable shift in the marketplace that collapses sales and puts the organization on the brink of bankruptcy, causing severe stress for everyone. A badly designed, badly programmed, badly implemented computer system or management-information system can create a data quagmire that leaves people blaming each other for providing poor information. Whatever the reason that widespread "blame" replaces "problem solving," it all boils down to one thing: the people doing the blaming feel trapped. They feel trapped because they cannot understand the problems affecting them and see no resolution. Or they feel that others are not cooperating to help resolve problems. Perhaps they feel that the problem is too large to be resolved or that there are too many problems to overcome. Whatever the case, they become apathetic and frequently resort to blame as a way of coping with the feeling that they are trapped in a box with no way out.

That feeling of being trapped is not conducive to problem solving, so problems mount. A mountain of unresolved problems overwhelms even the hard working employees. What one cannot handle, one avoids. Instead of taking responsibility, they start to blame co-workers, management, the customers, and the company itself. The issue of "blame" replacing "problem solving" usually builds up over time and is a sure sign that the organization is not resolving problems as a matter of routine.

Example: A confectionary manufacturer, who was also a distributor, was in deep functional trouble. Its computer system was full of problems, policies did not align the organization into a smooth operating unit, deliveries were severely messed up, executives were hired and fired routinely, production was way down, and customers were complaining bitterly. The company was losing money.

This situation continued for several years. The foreign parent company was screaming at the domestic operation for results and profits. Since no one in the organization knew or understood the black hole-creating items mentioned in this book, the company could not resolve the root causes. Blame was rampant. Managers blamed staff; staff blamed managers. The foreign parent company blamed the domestic operation; the domestic operation blamed the parent company. Things failed to improve and the functioning of the organization deteriorated to the point where the foreign parent decided to replace it.

xvii)   Good People Leave the Organization

The vast majority of good employees will tolerate an out-of-control, blame-ridden, chaotic environment for only so long before they look elsewhere for employment. For some reason, the not-so-good employees are more than happy to remain in a poorly functioning environment. Perhaps they enjoy "wallowing in the mud," as one close associate puts it. Given that humans are the most valuable aspect of most organizations, not much is left behind when good people leave bad organizations.

Example: A manufacturer of high-end luggage was in turmoil because management had allowed a black hole to form and then had done nothing about it for years. Many of the items that create black holes were eating away at the functioning of the organization and at the good employees. There was no visible improvement, so key personnel began to leave one by one. As they offered departing handshakes, they would say they were leaving "for a change," "for a better opportunity," "to work closer to home," "to be part of a more exciting industry," or "to semi-retire." However, they would confide to a select few that their departure was in response to the deteriorating functional condition of the organization. They did not want to work in that environment.

xviii)   Too Many Routine Items Become Projects

If there is a black hole, items that should be routine, such as installing curtain rods, become huge projects due to a breakdown in routine actions. Simple tasks or actions become frustrating time wasters and consume enormous resources.

Example 1:   The salesperson scribbled the order in poor handwriting; the installer went to the wrong address, at the opposite side of town.

Example 2:   Packing packed the wrong curtain rod model. The driver delivered it. After noticing the mistake, the driver had to pick up the right model, deliver it, and return the wrong model to the shop, where it had to be repackaged.

Example 3:   Nobody phoned the customer to ensure she would be home when the delivery was due. She was not. The driver had to return another day.

Example 4:   The installer was at the house next door that morning; with better planning, he could have performed installations in both houses during the same trip.

xix)   Too Many Variables Hamper Performance

When on site during a streamlining project, we sometimes lend the chief financial officer a diagram that highlights a concept we wish to keep in mind during the streamlining process.

The diagram above illustrates the following concept: organizations come into being to produce a good or provide a service in a manner that can be differentiated from that of the competition. Over time, because of the location, equipment used, policies or procedures adopted, processes implemented, and human abilities acquired, the organization develops a "sweet spot," a groove or flow—a way of doing something very well. To stay current or to match opportunities in the marketplace, that sweet spot might have been modified over time. It exists even though it may need to be slightly or dramatically improved.

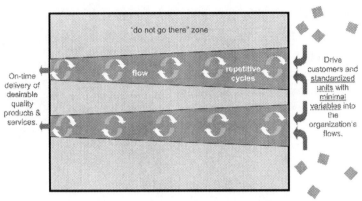

"do not go there" zone

On-time
delivery of
desirable
quality
products &
services.

flow

repetitive
cycles

Drive
customers and
standardized
units with
minimal
variables into
the
organization's
flows.

Limited Resources: time, labour, capital and materials.

Diagram courtesy of Corporate Streamlining Technology Inc.

The point of the diagram is to illustrate the importance of knowing the organization's sweet spot and driving both customers and other standardized units into it, or into the flow. Doing so makes it possible to lower costs, increase quality, improve delivery times, meet or exceed customer expectations, and so on. For instance, the use of standardized units, such as standard work-order and branch product requests, can reduce the number of different types of actions within the organization. A reduction in the number of different types of actions causes work to flow more smoothly. That, in turn, leads to tremendous efficiency gains and boosts organizational functionality and effectiveness.

The importance of reducing excessive randomness, or boosting standardization in organizations, permeates the streamlining process and is further illustrated above in section vi "Data Is Unstable" and section vii "Opportunities for Standardization Are Missed."

Increased demands on employees to multitask can be a symptom that a black hole exists, especially in large, mature organizations.

Example: An industrial materials producer had acquired heavy-duty processing equipment over time and aligned this equipment into a flow to produce an array of products. Each piece of expensive equipment could produce a range of products and had a preferred operating range with high processing speeds and optimized quality. In short, the process flow of this organization could satisfactorily produce a range of quality industrial materials. However, the sales department, supported by key senior executives, continually brought customized sales orders and potential sales orders to the vice president of operations and asked him to produce these similar yet different products.

This seemingly simple degree of randomness ballooned considerably, and the ramifications were felt in several parts of the company. Engineering would be called in to try to produce these new materials. To do so, they would be taken off their work of improving production processes and lowering the costs of producing existing products. Quality control would be pulled away from valuable quality control work on existing orders to see if the company could produce these new products to the customers' and company's quality standards. Expensive equipment and operators were taken offline for pilot testing of new products whenever such orders reached the plant floor, slowing production of existing orders. And sales clerks and managers stopped selling in order to figure out how to price these new orders, at least as a first approximation.

Excessive randomness was introduced into this company for little or no gain, since the company was already producing twenty-four hours per day, seven days per week, with an order book backlogged for several months. The new orders being considered were not large orders, and many were one-time orders. By considering these unusual orders, the company would not be breaking through into any new markets. Why engage in excessive randomness that immediately slows productivity, and chews away at the functionality of an organization in other ways over the long run, when there is no upside?

xx)   Number of Complaints Is Unacceptable

Needless to say, excessive customer and/or supplier complaints will arise when a black hole is present. They are bound to, because customers and suppliers are significantly affected by black holes in organizations with which they are conducting business. But while a high volume of customer and/or supplier complaints can be a manifestation of a black hole, not all such situations are black hole related. Many customer and/or supplier complaints arise because of numerous other failures.

If doubling or tripling the size of the customer service department to handle the growth in complaints is warranted, it should only be warranted in the short-term, because it is a rearguard action of containment that does not by itself resolve the root causes of these complaints. On the other hand, the collection of customer service data and the knowledge of customer service personnel *can* lead one to the root causes. Eventually the root causes themselves need to be terminated or the destructive cycle will not end, unless customers or suppliers terminate their business dealings with the organization.

Example: A home workshop distribution and installation company found itself the recipient of a growing number of customer complaints. Viewing this as a customer service issue only, management doubled the size of the customer service department. The customer service manager implemented procedures on how to handle phone calls from customers: for example, be honest and tell them their workshop would arrive late and then give them the revised estimated time of arrival and installation. The manager also asked the customer service personnel to personally arrange the shipment of missing and replacement parts to customers by courier.

Doubling the size of the customer service department was not enough, and customer complaints continued to grow, although the customers were very grateful for the manner in which complaints were acted upon by customer service staff.

The customer service manager was concerned about the growing workload of his newly expanded department. It had doubled in size, and yet his department was tapped out again. He was also concerned that the organization was receiving so many complaints. He investigated the situation and discovered numerous black hole-creating items further up line. The root causes of these issues were not being identified, handled, and eliminated. Root causes included shipping the wrong product, shipping damaged product, shipping product with parts missing, and product failing in the field after only a few months. As a result, his department was hit daily with a tidal wave of customer complaints. Actually, it was worse than a tidal wave, since tidal waves pass. This onslaught was constant.

xxi)   Number of Non-Routine Meetings Is Excessive

Holding an excessive number of non-routine meetings is actually an attempt to obtain routine data that is missing as a result of the many breaks in the organization. They may also be required to launch routine or heroic actions needed because other routine actions have fallen by the wayside, the subsequent damage is now apparent, and it must be handled immediately.

In the course of normal operations, meetings are required to strategize changes

in operations, to gain efficiency and effectiveness, to communicate management's vision and programs to employees, to praise employees for a job well done, to determine how to best prospect new leads, etc. There are other reasons why an organization requires meetings during normal operations, but it is an *excessive* number of meetings that forms part of the black hole landscape. Where a black hole is present, an excessive number of meetings is required to slow the rate of internal deterioration, rather than to foster better efficiencies and conquer new frontiers. Excessive meetings are a desperate attempt at survival.

Example 1:   The accounting manager for a natural gas supplier would become furious at month end when a series of management reports was due. At times, he would call five or six meetings per day, as he sent his accounting troops to the source documents, journal entries, and ledgers to piece together "best we can do, boss" data, requested by the accounting manager. This data was required to complete the management reports that the broken management information system was unable to produce readily.

Example 2:   When he discovered that the daily environmental procedures had been dropped many months earlier, the president of a manufacturing company held a series of emergency meetings with the vice president of operations, the quality control manager, two foremen, and others. The series of meetings continued until the president was certain every environmental procedure put in place by the company and its consultants was again being executed daily. The meetings continued until the president was certain he had discovered what had occurred to put society, as well as the company, officers, directors, employees, suppliers, customers, creditors, and shareholders, at risk. The culprit in this situation was the same one we often see when organizations turn into "water balloons": laziness, forgetfulness, assigning actions and programs to people with low responsibility levels, and a lack of controls to maintain program integrity.

xxii)   Financial Position Is Deteriorating

Although a deteriorating financial position can be the result of a long-existing black hole, there are other possible reasons, including market shifts, diminished ability to raise capital, and long-term contracts that are not re-negotiated, among others. Conversely, booming sales can temporarily disguise the existence of the "financial position is deteriorating" aspect of black holes.

So, one must be cautious when concluding that a deteriorating financial position is the result of a black hole. Having inserted that caveat, we will say that a deteriorating financial position is often present, or will be eventually, when a black hole is present. This is easy to understand when one understands that black hole-creating items are impediments to the functioning of the organization.

Example 1:   Failure to clearly state the scope of work for jobs that contractors were bidding on resulted in inconsistent bid submissions, numerous change orders being submitted by winning contractors, and subsequent project cost overruns.

Example 2:   The parking lot, offices, and plant of a custom furniture manufacturer were growing overcrowded with new full-time and temporary employees. Nobody identified the many black hole-creating items; their root causes were not terminated. Productivity was down and the plant required more and more employees to perform more and more work to achieve the same production levels. Costs rose because of this, and margins and profits sank. Cash flow and other financial numbers also deteriorated.

xxiii)   Deadlines Are Continually Missed

It only makes sense that deadlines will be missed if backlogs are present, handoffs are untimely, data is of poor integrity, good people have left the organization, items that should be routine have become time-consuming projects, and an excessive number of variables complicates the flows within the organization. Deadlines for delivery, accounting month-end closing, management reporting, production, bill payment, bank reconciliation, cash collection, government filing, project execution, and budget development can be missed because of black hole-creating items.

Example 1: The scheduler of an industrial processor found her job frustrating and complicated, despite having good scheduling software to work with. The inside sales clerk rarely had her final orders ready and submitted to the scheduler by the deadline. The scheduler then did not have adequate time to manage her preloads and to issue finished production schedules. Often, after the schedule was published to the plant, the inside sales clerk would send the scheduler additional orders, which in many cases were large or rush orders. The scheduler would have to reshuffle the schedule and try to catch orders before they were worked on in the plant. Sometimes, she would have to halt orders already in production. The source of all this grief was not the inside sales clerk. It was a lack of knowledge. The sales clerk *did not know* she had to get all orders to the scheduler by three o'clock each day.

Example 2: Distributors across the nation were in near riot mode because a manufacturer could not deliver plumbing fixtures on time. Late deliveries meant lost customers, and losing a builder was a serious matter. Builders saw their tradesmen standing around being paid union wages when the required material was a thousand miles away, and many builders had contracts allowing them to demand that the distributor pay a financial penalty for contract default. In addition to paying idle tradesmen, builders found it difficult to reschedule work, so late deliveries were a serious matter. In this example, continued late deliveries even had the potential to break the company.

xxiv) Responsibility Has Withered

Present deep within black holes is the manifestation of withered responsibility. Like a waitress who says "not my section" when she sees a spill across the room, employees who have withdrawn take responsibility only for the workflow right in front of them—no earlier and no later—rather than assist with the miles of *flow* within an organization.

The best organizations are far from perfect, and few if any organizations will ever line up so perfectly that every action runs flawlessly into or up against the next action all the time. Only in an ideal organization—one that exists in our imaginations—can organizations function with all cogs meshing seamlessly. Organizations are not composed of cogs but rather of functioning, thinking beings. To function smoothly, organizations need employees who consider the stations, situations, activities, or functions prior to and subsequent to their own. Views must overlap to make things run smoothly, to catch errors, and to spot opportunities. Understanding what the next person needs, why she needs it, and when she needs it can alter one's preparation and delivery of it.

Anyone assigned a function must have a view of that function. The person assigned to the previous function must have a view of the next function as well. And the person assigned to the following function must have a view of the previous function. So, at a bare minimum, each function should be viewed to some degree by at least three people—four, if we include the

supervisor. Now we are starting to gain some control over the organization. Now disconnects begin to be re-connected. Now we have a healthy situation in which the organization has the ability to repair itself.

These are not idle considerations. The ability to self-repair is a gift, a boon to the concept of organizations. Imagine the shape of organizations if it were not this way. It would be a shame to let this gift slip through one's fingers. *Removing black holes in organizations would dramatically improve an organizations ability to self-repair.*

Example: The scheduling supervisor of a very busy manufacturer knew why work orders flowed so haphazardly through the offices and the plant. The organization was in trouble, badly broken by black hole-creating items. This floundering was threatening his paycheck, yet the scheduling supervisor said nothing. Much false data was being spread around about procedures and actual workflows, and there was much blame and backstabbing. The vice president of production put up barriers and resistance to anyone offering suggestions. The scheduling manager committed a destructive act: he withheld the knowledge required to solve the problem and save this corner of the organization. Eventually, a contractor started to ask questions. The scheduling manager, under his breath, disclosed the problem and a potential solution to the contractor.

The contractor approached other key players one by one and casually bounced around the scheduling manager's solution. One at a time, they "saw the light" and started to fill in gaps in the process on their own, and even began to present their own solutions to the contractor. Once the contractor had the key players in agreement independently, he brought them together in pairs. They had to agree with each other at this point, because they had started to implement "their" solutions. The contractor discussed the improving situation with the vice president of operations. He co-opted the solution as his own and gave the contractor permission to rally the troops to implement "his" solution, which the contractor did by bringing all of the other parties together for a meeting. What a complex and convoluted way to solve an important and pressing problem. It could have been solved much more easily, but withering responsibility got in the way.

xxv)   Crib Notes Are Holding the Organization Together

Manually prepared notes on what to do when certain events happen (or do not happen) are a common and visible manifestation of black holes. These notes are not found in procedural binders; rather, they are the yellow sticky notes smothering computers, as well as the scraps of paper under keyboards and in drawers. These crib notes hold some organizations together.

Most organizations that have black holes for some time also have heroes within their ranks that management is likely unaware of. These heroes possess a high degree of responsibility, something opposite to the "withered responsibility" mentioned above. They have taken it upon themselves to do all they can to hold the organization together and to help it function. And what they have done in many cases is to bridge gaps between the organization's policies and procedures— with yellow sticky notes.

This process is rarely elegant, but it is often effective. And these heroes do it at a cost, often a heavy toll they place on themselves. The results are lost productivity and eventually burnout, as these heroes take time out from what they need to do to perform this patchwork.

Relying on heroes should only be a short-term fix—like NASA relied on the astronauts of *Apollo 13* to produce a patchwork fix that allowed the malfunctioning spacecraft to make it back to earth when the flight seemed doomed. You cannot hold an organization together forever with patchwork fixes. More permanent corrective actions must be implemented.

I hope no manager forgets to thank the heroes within the organization.

Example: The chief financial officer of a major carpet distributor wanted to know why a customer was not paying his large, past-due accounts receivable balance. He began his investigation by paying a visit to the accounts receivable clerk handling that account. From her drawer, the clerk pulled chargebacks that the customer had submitted—two co-op advertising charge-backs and one large charge-back for returns.

She then referred the chief financial officer to the "yellow stickies," as she called them, stuck on her computer. One read "co-op" at the top and listed the names and extensions of marketing managers responsible for making co-op advertising deals with customers, according to information provided to the clerk by the customer. The accounts receivable clerk then referred the chief financial officer to a second yellow sticky that read "returns" at the top. It listed two warehouse workers who received and counted product returned by the customers for credit. This yellow sticky also had the name and the phone number of the warehouse manager, while other yellow stickies had lists of quantities of products returned by various customers.

The accounts receivable clerk explained that customers frequently refused to pay invoices until they received a credit note for co-op advertising previously agreed to with a marketing manager, or for product returns. She had informed the respective managers of the customers' request for credit notes, but credit notes had not yet been issued.

The yellow stickies had become an integral part of the organization, filling a vacuum in the company's policies and procedures and workflow. The yellow sticky crib notes were the conduits through which company actions and the customer demands for credits met and were eventually resolved, actions such as making co-op advertising deals with customers and implementing a policy of accepting returned goods from customers in return for credit.

xxvi)   Same Time-Consuming Actions Are Surfacing

When root causes are not terminated, we see that the same time-consuming actions keep surfacing.

This item is similar to the one described in section xviii, "Too Many Routine Items Become Projects," except in this case, we are referring to items not so large as to become projects but repetitive enough to deserve our attention. Repetitive re-pricing of orders because of an unclear price model or unclear contract is a good example of this.

Example: Production personnel at a medium-sized metal fabricating shop would receive work orders every few weeks, specified in imperial measure when all of their standards, charts, and working tools were in metric. Each machine operator had to struggle on his own to calculate the conversions to metric. This meant machine downtime and errors, especially with respect to tolerances allowed. Somewhere, in the flow of work prior to the orders reaching the plant floor, the orders should have been converted to metric. My personal preference would have been for the sales department to handle the conversion by sitting with the customer, sorting out the conversions and agreeing on the values, and using these agreed-upon values in the contract. By doing this, the customer would have borne the risk of a wrong conversion, the organization would have had clean data entering its system, and the operators could have operated the machines instead of trying to finish off the sales order for the sales department.

xxvii)   The Ship Is Directionless

People, especially dedicated employees, like to work toward something. That is why a directionless ship is hard on morale, in addition to being wasteful of resources.

An organization with any reasonable plan is significantly more powerful than an organization without a plan or a goal or a dream. It is a strange thing, but even a seemingly silly or unreasonable dream or direction is better than no direction at all. No dream means "no game," and without a game the players cannot be mobilized. Then, apathy sets in.

A lack of direction will leave employees reacting only to whatever comes their

way. They will never initiate worthwhile actions, never drive toward something, because there is nothing to drive toward—unless they can no longer stand floating aimlessly. Then they, themselves, fill the vacuum with mischievous schemes and activities, or create constructive direction in their small corner of the organization. The problem with even seemingly constructive action, however, is that ambitions or actions might conflict with one another and might not be in the best interest of the organization.

Having direction enables an organization to tap into its human resources. Imagine having three thousand employees constantly on alert for opportunities that support the stated direction, all while they perform their usual duties.

If the chief executive officer were to *announce and then continually reinforce* that the company's goal was to have the shortest and most reliable delivery time in the industry, I am sure employees from all corners of the organization would offer suggestions on how to achieve this—especially if a formalized communication tool, such as a dedicated e-mail address, was provided.

There are at least four functions required to avoid this black hole-creating item. Omitting any one of these functions can impair organizations:

1. Management must develop direction for the organization.

2. Management must clearly communicate that direction to employees.

3. Management must continually reinforce that direction among the employees

4. Management must ensure that the direction is operationalized throughout the organization.

Without clear direction, employees have little motivation to apply their creative talents. Therefore, it would be fruitful for management to indicate to the organization the direction it should take. Otherwise, management will learn first hand what a black hole looks like when a few creative employees take it upon themselves to fill the void and do what suits them, which is not necessarily what suits the organization.

Example: Good people employed by a board game manufacturer and distributor acted badly because the organization was directionless. They were in no way malicious; they simply underutilized their talents because they had little opportunity to apply them. About the only work they did was to react to work that hit their desk. These were potentially very good employees, but the chief executive officer had no vision for his company, no direction, no plan. He too seemed to simply react to customers' requests and demands. The existing staff had no difficulty performing the work required, because the volume was modest and the work was fairly straightforward, but their abilities were severely underutilized.

xxviii) An Informal System Is In Operation

The dynamics of black holes in organizations allow informal systems to operate within formal systems more readily. Two main factors contribute to this:

1. The chaotic environment within black holes acts as a smokescreen behind which devious informal systems can operate.
2. The informal systems need to fill the vacuum of failed processes, policies and procedures of the formal system so the organization can still function, at least at some level.

You might have noticed from the above two factors that informal systems can  be constructive or destructive. Section xxv, "Crib Notes Are Holding the Organization Together", describes, in more detail, the workings of one particular constructive informal system— one that should not exist for long lest it collapse under its own weight. Section xxi, "Number of Non-Routine Meetings Is Excessive", describes an often-constructive system that exists to counter black hole-creating items. Talking with personnel removed from one's area of responsibility can also be constructive. Hearing gossip also exists, but this is often a destructive informal system.

The overlying trouble with an informal system operating within a formal system (or, more correctly, in place of a formal system) is that attention goes to the wrong place. Instead of going to the formal system and making it work better, attention is dispersed among informal systems. By nature, informal systems have less potential to be efficient and effective than formal systems do. That is why people commit great effort to constructing formal systems.

Example 1:   It took a click of the handcuffs to finally change the flow between a large natural gas producer and one of its large distributors. An informal system had replaced a director-sanctioned formal system of controls and approvals at one of the company's gas plants.

The informal system actually extended to the head office, where senior executives would tell the plant manager to sign contracts far in excess of the plant manager's signing authority. The informal system was a "boys' club," operating largely by verbal authorizations rather than the formal written-authorization system. When fraud was detected involving the plant manager and the distributor, the informal system was shut down. However, top executives escaped unscathed.

Does this sound familiar? It is what occurs in organized crime, where the top boss never puts in writing orders to commit crimes and never gets directly involved in the mechanics of the crime. He shields himself from the authorities so that when things go wrong, he is protected. In this case, the highest level executives, the real guilty parties issuing the verbal orders, were shielded from prosecution.

Example 2:   The board of directors at a community association was a board in name only. The strong-willed executive director wanted to run the show, and she did. Despite their legal obligations as board members, the board allowed the executive director to set strategy, set the annual budget, and refuse to give board members requested documents. The board also allowed the executive director to kill any board initiatives she was opposed to. A little research revealed the executive director had been put in place by a powerful group with vested interests. The weak board was her fodder. The informal system allowed the association to exist for the benefit of the vested interests, rather than for the public interests.

xxix)   Management Dreams of a Single "Big Hammer" Solution

When a black hole chews away at an organization for several years, the organization will experience many functional problems and operational difficulties. Such organizations experience many known problems that management does not have answers to or that they cannot get to in a timely manner. Layered on top of all this are the problems that management suspects exist but cannot identify. And then there are the problems that management is completely unaware of. This atmosphere is not conducive to stellar performance. In fact, it suppresses management. When people are suppressed, they sometimes dream of escaping to a remote island somewhere in the Caribbean to flee the pressures. Senior executives are no exception. Senior executives are subject to the same pressures of everyday life and the work world that we all are subject to, and sometimes those pressures can be unbearable—especially if one must report to a faraway parent company that only understands increased short-term profits.

But not everybody can walk away. Often, a reality in the presence of significant black holes is that management dreams of finding a single "big hammer" solution to all the organization's many problems. Buried by complexities, inconsistencies, and recurring problems, and squeezed by superiors, management seeks a quick solution—a ninth-inning home run, an overtime goal, a late-in-the-game Hail Mary touchdown pass.

You know what is occurring here. These are signs of desperation. All the accounting magic has been pulled out of the hat just to squeak through the next month, or the next quarter, and now management has run out of tricks and Band-Aid solutions. Not all black holes exert such dire pressure upon senior executives, but left undiscovered and unhandled long enough, they will.

Example: It had been going on for many years—a slow grinding deterioration of the functioning of the organization. Yet, management could not see it, or at least head office could not see it, for head office executives were only looking at numbers. They did not diagnose the inner workings of the organization. They did not look into its functionality (and when functionality deteriorates, the numbers will eventually deteriorate; however, the time lag can be substantial—especially if market conditions are good).

So, after all the extra effort by the employees to shore up the functional weaknesses and to make things work, and after all the accounting mirages had been used up, the numbers started to deteriorate. The deterioration of the organi-zation's functional health was severe, and the numbers got worse and worse. Local management fired this person and that person and gave a pep talk to this group and that group, but the numbers continued to slide.

Then local management started to look behind the numbers and began seeing broken processes and disconnects and dropped balls that created black holes. This caused them to panic. They sought a single "big hammer" solution—the old reliable "let's replace the system" solution that is so often the wrong one. One thought and *bam!* Problem gone. Or so management hoped. This was not the best way to terminate their black hole problems. In fact, the "solution" they came up with made things much worse for many reasons, including the fact that it simply calculated the wrong answers faster. Inevitably, the organization had to undergo a tremendously expensive and disruptive re-engineering to repair the damage.

xxx)   Alignment Is Poor

"Alignment is poor" means the actions that make up the organization are poorly arranged and out of synchronization. Organizations usually have the best chance of survival, and generally best serve society, when they consist of many repetitive actions. Repetitiveness increases the worker's confidence in what he is doing and subsequently reduces error rates. Repetitiveness also fosters reduced processing time. These repetitive actions can lose their appeal if any black hole-creating items work against them—break them down, cause them to slow down or misalign. A misalignment at the lower level usually also causes a break in the organization's larger repetitive actions.

Example 1: The budget of a custom manufacturing plant was not aligned to the plant output matrix. This meant the sales forecast used in the budget was unattainable at the plant level because of the limitations of the plant's capacity. The sales forecast was further unattainable because the sales were not broken down to the level at which the plant manager knew which machines could be used to satisfy the orders. The booked sales orders bottlenecked at certain machines, creating a severe backlog. Orders were subsequently cancelled as some machines remained idle.

Example 2: Company executives made no attempt to manage contribution margin. They did not assign responsibility for contribution margin to any executive or manager during the budget process and they made no attempt to track actual contribution margin anywhere within the organization at any level lower than monthly, which they rarely looked at. Likely, they made no attempt to manage contribution margin because not enough data was available, and the data that was available was often not reliable enough. As a result, and since the costing system had been abandoned, there were no constraints to prevent the sales department from selling products for lower and lower prices. The plant produced around the clock but could not keep up with orders, and still the company lost money. And, there was no contribution margin data to help determine which orders to produce and which ones to cancel. Tired of feeding the company cash, the chairman of the U.S. parent company eventually shut down the plant.

Example 3: An upstart in the marketing department of a consumer products manufacturer had a hot idea for a promotion. The idea would build on the buzz of an event that had just occurred in the

marketplace, and it was a good one for increasing sales volume of two of the company's products. However, the marketing campaign did not align with the plant's schedule, and the plant had the necessary machines booked for existing orders during the same four-month window in which the marketing campaign would place increased demands on production. Marketing department talent and manpower were wasted creating and researching a plan that would never be executed.

xxxi)   Black Hole-Creating Items Are Considered Petty

One of the more fascinating items we find in exploring black holes is this: senior management might conclude that black hole-creating items are petty.

It is unfortunate when management draws that conclusion, because the items listed in appendix A have caused many organizations to collapse. Black holes are not a sexy topic; however they can be a career-ender.

Black holes are a drain on resources, including cash and manpower. Black holes put the organization's image at risk, because they can result in poor quality products or services, late deliveries, and higher prices to customers. And black holes create unnecessary complexity and *hide much larger problems and opportunities* and so are just as important as these larger items.

Black hole-creating items, by their very nature, prolong the time it takes until they are discovered and so prolong the period of losses. In addition to hiding problems outright, they potentially complicate, or even hide, the *anatomy* of larger known problems. In that way, black holes in organizations leverage and exacerbate the potential destruction that larger problems can cause. Discovering black hole-creating items, and terminating them, is often necessary to properly eliminate the larger problems, even if the larger problems are already known by management. It is one thing to know the organization has a problem and quite another to know the anatomy of that problem.

For any organization with at least mildly black-hole-free competition, that competition limits the amount the organization can charge for its goods and services. Therefore, if left unhandled long enough, black holes can grow to the point where they will drain the till dry, either directly or by complicating larger problems.

Some organizations with unhandled black holes chewing away at their resources and credibility are temporarily saved by an extremely tolerant marketplace that is willing to fund an organization's black hole, and this gives management a false sense of security. Sometimes, customers fund an organization's unhandled black holes by paying higher prices. At other times, creditors fund an

I wish we knew before what we know now.

organization's unhandled black holes by extending further credit. And at still other times, the shareholders forego dividends or supply more diluting share capital to re-engineer or replace the organization's entire computer system, even when that is not the main problem, or increase "working capital" for a few more years.

There are not many problems larger to an executive than a lack of return on capital.

Example: Late Learner Company rolled the dice, hoping everything was fine in the organization, and decided not to look behind the bushes and under the rocks. Management saw no visible smoke anywhere—just a little over here and a little over there, all part of business. It was petty. Late Learner Company had hired good people, so everything would be okay.

On October 14, Mrs. Customer did not receive her sofa on time, as promised, because there was a mild disruption when the receiver took control of the business.

Appendix B

(Reprinted with permission from Chartered Secretaries Canada,
www.icsacanada.org)

Good Governance Guides

Index of Good Governance Guides

As a service to members and others, Chartered Secretaries Canada has prepared a series of Good Governance Guides in the area of corporate governance. The intention is that they will provide value to individuals as a starting point or as an information source on governance issues.

In all instances, you should be complying with applicable legislation and case law but there are often grey areas not covered by legislation and practices in these areas can vary from minimal to best practice. These Guides comprise what, in our view, constitutes good governance in a range of situations. They are a guide only, not a substitute for seeking professional legal advice.

As a global professional organization, we are able to offer you, for comparison and further ideas, Good Governance Guides from each of the Divisions of ICSA.

1. Structure
    1.1   Board Charter
    1.2   Committees of the Board
    1.3   Composition and Size of the Board
    1.4   Independence of Directors

For further details, please visit www.icsacanada.org

Appendix C

Real Life Examples of Problems/Opportunities Unearthed While Addressing Black Holes in Organizations

Addressing black hole-creating items leads to the discovery, and potential resolution, of larger organizational gains. When one is deep in the belly of an organization and is working through, locating, and resolving black hole-creating items, one finds that larger problems and opportunities present themselves. This occurs for a few reasons:

1. Attention is being placed on areas that have, historically, received little attention.

2. The people working through, locating, and resolving black hole-creating items cross several departments and have a chance to view the entire organization. They gain a valuable perspective of the organization that few employees possess.

3. As the burden is cleared, as the number of variables is reduced, and as stability, rationality, consistency, and overall operational functionality increase, the organization becomes more transparent.

Below are a few representative samples covering a broad range of issues that we at Corporate Streamlining unearthed while addressing black holes in organizations:

1) Accounts Receivable

A company's accounts receivable ledger contained tens of thousands of entries. Thousands of these entries were non-standard. These entries would have impeded the conversion to a new accounting system in terms of conversion processes and staff time.

Corporate Streamlining adjudicated thousands of non-standard items in various ways, usually after investigating each item—or group of items—and pulling documents to support the receivable items if documents were available. Additionally, we prepared cases for staff to negotiate with customers.

Customer back charges, unpaid balances, misapplied cash, unsupportable invoices, incorrect pricing, unsupportable journal entry items, disputed commission amounts, and other trouble items were cleaned up.

We created a clean accounts receivable sub-ledger that had integrity and was ready to be rolled into the new computer system.

2) Pricing

A company was about to embark on a large computer conversion program. Problems in the pricing department created month-end closing delays that would have fouled the conversion process. Month-end reporting rarely closed on time. By re-sequencing the flow of work orders, the pricing department did not have to search for missing work orders at month end, and so month-end reporting closed on time from then on. Thus, the company was able to avoid any headaches resulting from such a conversion.

3) Unpleasant Surprises

Corporate Streamlining developed and implemented an effective monthly management report system that contained special characteristics customized for the company so that senior management was no longer caught by surprise.

4) Workflow Data Integrity

Almost ten thousand work orders were not advanced in the company's existing workflow management system, and the system was about to be replaced. The existing workflow management system was reviewed and departmental reports were printed. These reports listed the work orders supposedly in each department. However, very few of the work orders were in the departments, as most of them had been completed or cancelled. We worked with the departments to close the completed and cancelled work orders that were still on the system and to leave the active work orders on the system. Only active work orders remained, ready to be rolled into the new computer system. The company could then launch its new system with an accurate view of work orders.

5) Policies

A re-engineering project had commenced, but it was moving forward slowly. The company had not yet decided if it was a custom manufacturer or a standard product manufacturer, or if it wanted to be a hybrid of the two.

Corporate Streamlining pushed the importance of having a clear vision, so management analyzed the situation more closely and determined where on the "custom versus standard" spectrum the company should be positioned. Once they determined their position, the re-engineering process went much more smoothly.

6) Invoice Price Verification

A company was manually verifying the prices on hundreds of invoices received weekly from a major supplier. We designed an automated system for verifying the prices and asked staff to program it into Microsoft Access. Once automated, the workload was reduced by 75 percent. Additionally, because of this program, the company discovered the vendor's pricing model to be incorrect. The company notified the vendor who, in turn, made the appropriate corrections.

7) Plant Gains

After assessing a manufacturing situation, we provided plant personnel with a sledgehammer to help remove the mandrel (an axle used to secure or support material being machined or milled) from the machine. On average, this saved 30 minutes per mandrel change, according to the operator. Who says simple solutions are not effective?

8) Negotiations and Settlements

We were called in during tough negotiations between a manufacturing company and one of its important customers over money owed to the manufacturer by its customer. After assessing the situation and based on a blank-slate look at both sides of the issue, we prepared extensive background reports and proposed settlement packages totaling millions of dollars. Once the customer could see the justification for the outstanding charges, they were able to come to a mutually acceptable settlement with the manufacturer. The relationship between the two companies was saved, and the manufacturer altered the billing processes to avoid future disputes with their customers.

9) Payroll

Corporate Streamlining developed Excel spreadsheets to automate payroll buildup for plant personnel. Besides saving manual clerical time to prepare payroll, the company was able to realize huge savings in follow-up because the spreadsheet method virtually eliminated the vast number of manual errors being made.

10) Purchasing

After reviewing a problem-plagued purchasing department, we discovered serious weaknesses in purchasing procedures. So we drafted a purchasing manual for management to review and approve, and for purchasing personnel to use. As purchasing began to follow specific, standardized procedures, the problems disappeared. The purchasing manual was branded "good work" by all who used it— including management, who had fewer fires to douse.

11) Purchasing

We saw the potential for huge efficiency gains in the requisitioning, purchasing, and accounts payable cycles of one company. Initially, we created a series of purchase requisitions in Excel. These requisitions became purchase orders, and then they were converted into packing slips. Finally, they were processed as receiving documents that were then matched to the original purchase order by accounts payable, prior to paying invoices. This method greatly reduced the time required to prepare purchase orders and increased the accuracy of the purchase orders. It also reduced the time needed to verify complex invoices to near zero.

12) Operating Losses

A large plant was operating at full capacity—twenty-four hours per day, seven days per week—and it was losing money. Upon analysis, we discovered that the answer to this dilemma was rooted in an action that had occurred eight years ago.

At that time, management had terminated a procedure that was not fully understood, in an attempt to save money.

13) Inaction

Interdepartmental flow issues were not being handled well in a large organization, and that situation was creating problems. We developed a solution to this chronic problem. It involved understanding the workflow and then preparing a solution for all to follow. That solution, a routing form system, ensured that the right person—the person with problem-solving authority and responsibility—in the right department handled the right issue. Now, all routing forms are logged and a time-sensitive follow-up system is in place. If problems are not solved within a defined timeframe, senior management receives a report and can take action. In other words, the solution was a closed system. Once an issue is identified, it cannot be ignored or forgotten about and left to clog the organization. It can only be handled. The routing form system has been implemented by Corporate Streamlining twice, both times with stellar results.

14) Environment

Upon inspection, we discovered that a company's daily environmental checklist had not been used in five months. Employees hid behind a veil of ignorance—they did not understand the system or its implications. This put the company, its officers, and its directors at serious financial and legal risk. The company recommenced using the daily environmental checklist and made the documentation available to government inspectors.

15) Distribution Agreement

A company did not have a formal framework or standardized rules for dealing with its distributors, who numbered over one hundred. You can imagine the inconsistency and rancor between the company and some of its distributors. More importantly, the lack of formal agreements was a hidden potential time bomb that left the door wide open for all the distributors to leave for another manufacturer at once. We identified the problem and then drafted a distribution agreement for legal vetting and management review.

16) Manpower

Staffing, a lack of staff, or ways to cut staff are often issues within organizations. This is particularly the case when the productivity of staff cannot be measured, or when inefficient workflow causes backlogs and bottlenecks. We resolved the issue of a pricing manager's continuous requests for more staff by (1) analyzing the productivity level of all pricing staff; (2) discovering underused personnel; (3) formulating better company procedures; (4) standardizing documents flowing into pricing; and (5) pushing incomplete work flowing into pricing from other departments back to the departments from which the incomplete work originated.

17) Organizational Readiness

Management of a company was convinced that the company was ready for a large-scale computer conversion and company-wide re-vamping. Corporate Streamlining showed them otherwise and then set out to increase the company's readiness. Although we did not see the completion of the project (as that was not our mandate), the gains we made by readying the organization to move forward made the project personnel's job much easier. Increasing the company's readiness also improved the results of the project. In addition, we greatly reduced the volume of *dirty data* in the company that would have encumbered the new system. As a result, future write-offs decreased. By increasing the company's readiness, the likelihood of success for the overall project increased.

18) A Warning Unheeded

Corporate Streamlining observed that a company's products were deteriorating in quality and that quality control mechanisms were not being diligently followed. We presented a hypothetical probability distribution curve that stressed how the chances of undesirable events occurring had increased dramatically because quality control mechanisms were not being followed. The company took no significant quality control action, and within two months, an Asian customer refused nine shipping containers of custom product. Furthermore, the company's largest Canadian customer refused its largest shipment of the year.

19) Credit and Collections Policies and Procedures

As it did in the "Purchasing" scenario, Corporate Streamlining discovered serious weaknesses in an organization's credit and collections policies as well as procedures that put it at risk. There were also issues concerning credit granting, cash application, and collection. We drafted the company's *Credit and Collections Policies and Procedures Manual* for customer management review and approval and for credit department personnel to use to alleviate these issues.

20) Premature Invoicing

Corporate Streamlining identified that a company was issuing millions of dollars' worth of invoices prior to completion of the work. This arrangement was causing friction with customers. We designed a procedure that would not permit invoicing until work was signed "completed" by the customer.

21) Cash Application

An organization was improperly applying cash application repeatedly to customer accounts receivables because of certain complexities. We developed a customer payment breakdown template in Excel to streamline the flow and to properly process these complexities. This system greatly facilitated cash application and reduced future write-offs significantly.

22) Claims for Credits

As standard operating procedure, a large-ticket item company issued invoices in multiple parts, usually three for each order (i.e., three separate invoices and credit notes). The three parts included basic price, credits, and re-bills for modifications. Customers immediately deducted credits for all purchases from their next payment, without making any payment on the debit portion of the invoices until months later. We worked with the IT department to issue one invoice for each order/shipment so that customers could not use the credit without also paying the invoice to which the credit related.

23) Gross Margins

Customer management had been operating on the assumption that gross margins were positive and healthy, when in fact the gross margins were negative. This discovery dramatically altered management's strategic plans.

24) Cash Flow

Customer management had been operating on the assumption that $40 million in accounts receivable, inventory, and accounts payable credits (total balances were much higher) could be turned into cash. In fact, this $40 million had to be written off. This information was significant. Management did not know the reality of the situation, thus, strategic plans were based on false assumptions. This new information dramatically altered management's strategic plans.

25) Root Causes

Corporate Streamlining attempts to identify and resolve root causes of issues. On one project, we identified fifty-four root causes in one department alone, many of which were procedural. Once the root causes were handled, the department went from being a weight on the organization to one that continually received praise from the president and senior executives of the parent company.

26) Annual Budget

Corporate Streamlining personnel took over the function of compiling the annual budget for two companies (a Canadian public company and a subsidiary of a U.S. public company). In both cases, we demonstrated that no one in these organizations was being held responsible for the most important yet most ignored financial number—the contribution margin (after direct and semi-direct costs are deducted from the selling price, it is the money left over to pay for overhead and to leave a profit). Therefore, the sales staff of one company was able to undercut the competition. They got away with it—until the company shut its doors.

Almost anything can come up during a project that addresses black holes in organizations. Some problems/opportunities are small and quick to handle, while others are more dramatic. The above are merely a few examples of the hundreds of problems and opportunities of varying importance that we have unearthed and resolved or presented to management for resolution, during our streamlining practice.

APPENDIX D

LETTERS

MCL GROUP INC.

664 McGeachie Drive, Milton, ON, Canada L9T 3Y5
TEL (905) 878-0083 FAX (905) 878-1824
TOLL FREE: 1-888-MCL-HEAT (1-888-625-4328)
www.mclgroup.biz

June 4, 2003

Mr. Ron Lutka
President
Corporate Streamlining Company Inc.
146 West Beaver Creek Road
Unit #2
Richmond Hill, Ontario
L4B 1C2

Subject: Corporate Streamlining Services

Dear Mr. Lutka:

We would like to thank Corporate Streamlining for assisting us with our computer conversion project and for handling the reconciliation of several difficult accounts that needed to be undertaken in our accounting department after our recent purchase of the company. In our discussions and in practice it became evident how Corporate Streamlining approaches improving organizations from the bottom up.

It is refreshing to see a consulting company, or as you say "a management services company" who is willing to roll up their sleeves and actually do the work not merely report on what needs to be accomplished. And it was refreshing to see how Corporate Streamlining approaches improving organizations differently from labour brokers who I have never seen bring a standardized streamlining technology to the table, although we realize we did not utilize Corporate Streamlining fully in this regard.

Thank you again, and we wish you well.

Regards,

Gary Crombie
Controller
MCL Heat Transfer Ltd.

Wolverine Ratcliffs Inc.

865 Gartshore Street, Fergus, Ontario, Canada N1M 2W7 TEL: (519) 843-2440 FAX: (519) 843-6087 SALES: 1-800-668-7265

January 26, 2001

RE: Mr. Ron Lutka, President
          Corporate Streamlining Company Inc.

To Whom It May Concern:

This letter will confirm Ron Lutka was employed by our Company from June 30, 2000 to January 26, 2001 on a consulting basis.

In this capacity he conducted a company wide business review after our company merged with Ratcliffs Severn Inc. Ron reviewed most of the company's departments and functions. He documented and made numerous recommendations and then teamed up with our Information Systems Manager to conduct a systems review.

Business Improvement Teams have been established that will incorporate these findings. Areas are; Accounting & Finance, Quality Control, Sales & Marketing, Purchasing, Inventory Management, Annual Budget, Standard Costing, Logistics, Production, Human Resources, Capital Projects, Engineering Maintenance and Hedging.

If you require further information do not hesitate to call our office.

Regards,

Robert Wordham
Chief Executive Officer

A WOLVERINE TUBE, INC. COMPANY

Ron Lutka worked as a consultant in a full time capacity at Canac (a division of Kohler Company) from June 2001 to October 31, 2002.

During that time Ron took on high priority projects for the Finance Department.

Ron's first mandate was to start working in the credit department, where it was identified that we had some serious process problems within our Accounts Receivable Department.

His results included the resolving of key accounts issues and the implementation of audit controls and reports.

Through Ron's focused drive for success, hard work, leadership, and depth of analysis along with problem solving skills and teamwork, the accounts receivable department was brought under control within 8 months.

Once Ron's mandate was over in the A/R department, I had assigned him to numerous other senior accounting and system related projects, where Ron applied his Corporate Streamlining Technology® resulting in material gains for Canac duly recognized by senior management at Kohler.

His enthusiasm and abilities to move from one duty to another and perform them well was impressive.

We would not hesitate to hire him again should the need arise.

Sincerely

Frank Sartor
Director Of Finance

Walter Ramka
Corporate Credit Manager

KOHLER CO. KOHLER, WISCONSIN 53044 PHONE 920-457-4441 www.kohlerco.com

KOHLER

April 2, 2002

Dear Ron:

Over the past few months, the credit and receivables personnel at Canac have faced the daunting task of bringing receivables under control. Walter Ramka and Frank Sartor have highly commended your efforts, and the results are becoming evident. We still have further work to do before we are at acceptable performance levels. However, first steps are crucial to our success.

Given the level of effort you have expended and the changes that we see, we would like to recognize your efforts and the results. With that in mind, attached you will find a brochure detailing Kohler's associate apparel collection. As a small token of our sincere appreciation for a job well done, please choose any item or items up to a total of $60. Once selected, please complete the attached order form and return it to Kohler Co., attention Kathy Lulloff. She will then order the items and have them shipped to you.

We look forward to further significant improvements in the months to come and are confident that with your drive, enthusiasm, and dedication that we will soon reach our desired goals at Canac. Thank you again and keep up the good work!

Sincerely,

Jeffrey P. Cheney
Senior Vice President - Finance

John M. Suralik
Treasurer

Delbert P. Haas
Vice President & Corporate Controller

Dean R. Wendt
Director - Corporate Credit

Mr. Ron Lutka
XXXXXXXXXXXXXXXXX
XXXXXXXXXXXXXXXXX
XXXXXXXXXXXXXXXXX

JPC/kl

HINO MOTORS CANADA, LTD.

396 AMBASSADOR DRIVE	PHONE: (905) 670-3062	MONTREAL OFFICE	CALGARY OFFICE
MISSISSAUGA, ONTARIO	FAX: (905) 670-3770	PHONE: (514) 919-0100	PHONE: (406) 275-0640
L5T 2J3	PARTS: (905) 673-3775	FAX: (514) 642-3100	FAX: (406) 275-0642
www.hinocanada.com	PARTS FAX: (905) 673-7405		

May 16, 2006

Re: Ron Lutka

To Whom It May Concern:

Ron Lutka joined us in 2005 on contract to function as the Controller of the company.

In that capacity he performed not only the controllership function but also many others relating to the improvement of business and accounting procedures.

Ron worked diligently and professionally. His list of accomplishments are substantial; and, the Company's procedures have been improved significantly.

It is important to note that Ron also achieved his objectives by working with the staff of the Company in a very professional manner. As a result he is highly regarded by everyone.

Sincerely,

Axel Breuer
Vice President Finance & Administration.

BEAMSCOPE ✳

July 21, 1999

TO WHOM IT MAY CONCERN:

Ron Lutka was brought in April of 1998 to handle special high level priority accounting projects for the Finance Department.

Ron started to work in the Credit Department shortly thereafter when it was identified that we had some serious process problems within our Accounts Receivable Department. Ron was responsible for a staff of over 10 Associates and 3 Team Leaders.

His responsibilities included the reconciliation of all our Key Accounts and the implementation of audit controls both in Accounts Receivable as well as Cash management. His key mandate was to identify and if possible reconcile all of our Key Accounts and report his findings to Senior Management.

Through Ron's hard work, leadership, analytical as well as problem solving skills he was able to bring the Accounts Receivable portfolio under control within 10 months.

Once Ron's mandate was over within the Credit Department, our C.F.O. assigned him to numerous other senior level accounting projects of which I understand he did an outstanding job.

I would highly recommend Ron to your organization at a Senior Accounting Management level.

Should you require additional information please do not hesitate to call me.

Walter A. Ramka
National Credit Manager
Beamscope Canada Inc.

Corporate Office
136 Yorkville Avenue
Second Floor;
Toronto, Ontario
M5R 1C2

Phone: 416.966.0000
Fax: 416.966.2700
EMail: info@beamscope.com

Eastern Canada
33 West Beaver Creek Road
Richmond Hill, Ontario
L4B 1L8

Phone: 905.763.3000
Toll Free: 1.800.268.5535
Fax: 905.763.3001
EMail: info@beamscope.com

Western Canada
12851 Rowan Place
Richmond, British Columbia
V6V 2K5

Phone: 604.821.0000
Toll Free: 1.800.268.3521
Fax: 604.303.2220
EMail: info@beamscope.com

Unisel Argentina
Pedro de Mendoza 679
1156 Buenos Aires
Argentina

Phone: 541.307.0874
Fax: 541.307.1043
EMail: info@unisel.com.ar

Unisel Chile
El Conquistador del Monte 4844
Huechuraba
Santiago, Chile

Phone: 562.740.0074
Fax: 562.740.0072
EMail: info@microcomp.cl

GLOSSARY

(Terms as they are used in this book)

backlog: Work that someone had the full intention or desire to complete but did not fulfill within a time frame that the business model demanded. It includes physical processing as well as conceptual work, such as realigning distribution channels.

big-change event: An event that causes a *sudden* change to the organization and is of such large magnitude that it rapidly disrupts the functioning of the organization, thus threatening its survival. This sudden change can be the result of an external force, such as a sudden shift in technology or industry specifications, or an internal force, such as an awkward software conversion.

"big hammer" solution: A derogatory term meaning an attempt by management to solve all or many of the organization's problems by way of a single thought, such as eliminating all middle managers or replacing the enterprise reporting system. It is a desperate attempt to save a troubled organization wrought with problems.

black hole: An area of an organization where, unbeknownst to management, an abundance of undesirable activities occurs or a lack of desirable activities occurs in abundance, either of which can destroy an organization.

black hole-creating items: Individual undesirable activities or individual lack of desirable activities unknown to management which, as a group, form a black hole.

Buffet, Warren: Born August 30, 1930, in Omaha, Nebraska, Mr. Buffett is an American investor, businessman, and philanthropist who amassed a personal net worth of \$42 billion by way of astute investing.[31]

break: *Micro*: a failure during the execution of an *action* for any of several reasons such as inadequate tools, inadequate training, misunderstood or no communication, intent to cause failure, or interruptions. *Macro*: a general failure in *organizational functionality*.

cog: A colloquial business term derived from the following dictionary definition: "A wheel or bar with projections on its edge, which transfers motion by engaging with projections on another wheel or bar".[32] It is any mechanical apparatus of a business. Not a human element.

Corporate Streamliner: A registered certification mark owned and issued by Corporate Streamlining Technology Inc. to streamliners who have achieved specified benchmarks.

Corporate Streamlining: Corporate Streamlining Company Inc., "operating as".

Corporate Streamlining Company Inc.: Currently, the sole legal entity that applies Corporate Streamlining Technology to organizations.

Corporate Streamlining Technology Inc.: The legal entity that holds the Corporate Streamlining Technology intellectual property and enforces standard application of Corporate Streamlining Technology by licensed users. It also administers the Corporate Streamlining Technology course and issues the Corporate Streamliner and CorpS certification marks.

Corporate Streamlining Technology: A registered certification mark owned by Corporate Streamlining Technology Inc. that signifies a methodology for evaluating the efficiency and effectiveness of an organization or parts thereof; also, a process for improving the efficiency and effectiveness of an organization or parts thereof.

CorpS: A registered certification mark owned and issued by Corporate Streamlining Technology Inc. to streamliners who have achieved specified benchmarks, but less so than a Certified Streamliner.

critical path: "A critical path is the path materials, documents, or thoughts and sometimes bodies flow along, usually containing a sequence of actions, which limits the speed of flow of the output of the overall organization. It is the path *limiting the overall flow*. The flow that restricts increased output of the organization. The degree to which the stops and hindrances along the critical path can be relieved is the degree to which overall output of the organization can be increased."[33]

disconnects: A permanently broken or intermittently broken routine flow *between* actions or people (as opposed to *within* an action). It could be a broken written or oral communication flow, a broken material flow, a broken product flow, a broken flow of bodies (as in a "no show" situation), or even a broken flow of thoughts or ideas.

dynamics (of organizations): Powerful forces that are inherent in all organizations; also, vital characteristics common to all organizations.

derivatives (financial): Financial instruments that depend on the performance of underlying financial instruments or assets for their value.

"end of the wisp": A slang term meaning late in the chain of cause and effect.

Enron Corporation: Corporate entity that filed for bankruptcy on December 2, 2001 (which is the largest bankruptcy filing in history to date), despite having a reported net worth of over US$10 billion. The reported net worth did not include off-balance sheet liabilities related to financial derivatives.[34]

entropy: A tendency toward disorder or randomness in an open system.

flow: (1) The continuous movement of materials, people, ideas, communications, money, or thoughts from one point to another, or (2) the continuous performance of a sequence of actions.

formal system: A system, or network of systems, within an organization that management has planned and implemented to achieve the organization's objectives.

incomplete work: Like backlog, incomplete work includes the failure to execute any action that would lead to the realization of the organization's goals. However, incomplete work and backlog differ because of intention. *Backlog*: someone intended to complete the work but did not for various reasons, such as not having time to draft a budget. *Incomplete work*: no one had the intention to complete the work, and it was not completed, for example, no one took the initiative to implement new packaging guidelines, or no one filed the burr off the cut acrylic before passing the material to the next station.

inconsistencies: Unnecessary differences in actions or communications; or in format, style, or medium, as items flow through the organization. Inconsistencies jam workflow because the inconsistencies must be reconfigured or analyzed each time before furthering the item along the line. Shipping goods to a terminal on forty-eight-inch skids that then have to be unpacked and loaded onto forty-two-inch skids before export is an example of an inconsistency.

informal system: A system that has developed on an ad hoc basis among employees without management's approval. The informal system can be constructive, because it makes up for deficiencies in the formal system, or destructive, because it circumvents the formal system and acts contrary to the organization's objectives. The trouble with an informal system operating in place of a formal system is that attention goes to the wrong place. Instead of attention going to the formal system and making it work, and work better, attention is dispersed into informal systems.

mechanical damage: Damage caused to the way the organization functions mechanically. Mechanical damage is low-end damage, but it is often broad and repetitive damage that, in the aggregate, leads to the failure of organizations. Example: wasting time obtaining specifications from engineers who have left the department, because the knowledge was not written into a manual or schedule prior to their departure.

open system: Internal energy can be released out of the system and external energy can enter the system. With reference to "syntropy" and "entropy," both energies can enter an organization from outside the organization. Likewise, both energies can exit the organization and affect entities outside the organization.

operationalize: To impart a thought into the physical world by initiating appropriate action in the physical world. More specifically, to impart a thought into the day-to-day workings of an organization by initiating appropriate action within the organization.

"organisms": Equivalent to life forms and therefore affected by much of what life forms are subject to. They react in a similar or identical way to life forms. They are able to create ideas, generate energy, cause things to occur, feel enthusiasm and become upset as life forms do.

"**pockets**": A grouping or collection of anything into a small area of the organization. Pockets can be desirable or undesirable. Undesirable pockets tend to form around breaks. Tasks can also pocket and become unevenly distributed among employees, as many small tasks can pocket onto one person's desk.

poor alignment: Actions designed to help the organization achieve its goals are poorly arranged and out of synchronization, thereby impairing the organization's ability to achieve those goals.

real gains: The results of actions that increase the probability of an organization attaining its goals. These gains are distinctly different from "reported gains" because reported gains might not be the result of any increase in the probability of an organization attaining its goals. Reported gains might be solely due to inaccurate reports.

results damage: Damage caused to an organization that can be expressed in terms of a failed goal or objective, or an increased risk of such failure.

root cause: The first working-level cause that, when working *backward* along the sequence of causes leading to an undesirable result, will end the undesirable result if addressed.

spirit ("broken"): A spirit is an entity that is not part of the physical universe but that, among other things, operates the human body to attain objectives in the physical universe. A "broken" spirit is one that has become lessened: less powerful, less effective, less useful, and/or less able to alter the physical universe. Therefore, it is less able to operate heavy machinery, to understand a customer's needs, to conduct a sound marketing campaign, and to receive and forward phone calls.

streamlining: The process of aligning an organization's thoughts, actions, and resources to best serve the goals of that organization.

structural damage: Damage caused to the organizational structure. The disruption of delivery to customers because of a drivers' dispute is an example of structural damage.

"**sweet spot**": Over time, because of the location, equipment used, technology possessed, policies or procedures adopted, processes implemented, and human abilities acquired, an organization develops a "sweet spot," a groove or flow—a way of doing something very well.

syntropy: A tendency toward harmonious association in an open system.

subtle factors: Used in reference to entropy. Subtle-factor entropy is the eating away of an organization slowly over time, causing the organization to deteriorate functionally, and eventually, financially.

"time bomb" (potential hidden): Within an organization, it is the existence of a potential event that is not readily visible and that can cause significant damage to the long-term survival or prosperity of the organization, should it occur.

*too **distant** in "mechanics":* As data is rolled up the information pyramid, there are several mechanical handlings of the data between the actual events and the point that the data is ready to be used to draw conclusions. These many handlings can cause the data to lose its integrity, usually because of the grouping of dissimilar data or errors in data compilation. The term is used in this book in reference to problems with many business-failure prediction models.

*too **distant** in "time":* A large amount of time elapses between the actual events and the point that the data is compiled and ready to be used to draw conclusions; this often happens with financial statements. These time lags can cause the data to lose value as the organization continues to change. The term is used in this book in reference to problems with many business-failure prediction models.

transparent (organization): Organizations can be transparent or opaque. Transparent organizations are easier to manage and to drive toward the organization's goals. On the other hand, trying to manage opaque organizations is like driving blind.

"trenches": Referred to as "middle-management trenches." It is a slang term meaning the mid-level of an organization, where there is a high volume of basic administration and execution activity. It is a brother of "weeds" (see definition in Glossary).

unstable data: Data that is neither strongly supported nor secured and, therefore, can be altered or even disappear in the face of entropy. Attention to data, manuals, training, good record keeping, notes, proper storage, reconciliation, and checklists help to stabilize data.

"wallowing in the mud": Slang term meaning being happy to exist in a chaotic environment over a long period.

"weeds": Referred to as "supervisory and worker" weeds. It is a slang term meaning the lower-level of an organization, where there is a high volume of detail. It is a brother of "trenches" (see definition in Glossary).

"withered responsibility": An unhealthy situation in which employees withdraw and no longer maintain a vigilant eye for opportunities and internal and external threats to the organization, including small breaks and failings. The employees have withdrawn and take responsibility only for the workflow in front of them—no earlier and no later—rather than assisting with the miles of *flow* within an organization, especially with regard to the activities preceding and following their own. When this occurs, an organization loses its ability to repair itself.

yellow sticky notes (or "yellow stickies"): Pieces of adhesive-backed paper on which employees, especially clerks, record data critical to the smooth operating of their function that are not contained in the organization's manuals. The bits of paper are often, but not always, yellow.

ENDNOTES

Chapter 1

1 *Oxford Dictionary of Current English,* 3rd ed. (New York: Oxford University Press, 2001), 84.

2 At the Seventeenth International Conference on General Relativity and Gravitation in Dublin, Ireland, in July 2004, physicist Stephen Hawking modified his thirty-year black hole theory, claiming that "mass energy will be returned but in a mangled form." 3 Mr. Hawking's modified definition of an astronomical black hole still sufficiently describes the nature of black holes in organizations. The fact that he modified his theory after thirty years supports the analogy, for as we will show, black holes in organizations are elusive.

3 Dr. David Whitehouse, "Black Holes Turned 'Inside Out'," *BBC News Online,* July 22, 2004, http://news.bbc.co.uk/1/hi/sci/tech/3913145.stm (accessed July 24, 2006).

Chapter 3

4 John R. Baldwin, *Failing Concerns* (Ottawa: Statistics Canada, 1997), 9.

Chapter 6

5 Celia Wolf and Paul Harmon, *The State of Business Process Management* (Newton, MA: Business Process Trends, 2006), 39.

6 Ibid.

Chapter 9

7 See appendix B, "Good Governance Guides".

Chapter 10

[8] In chapter 10 "organizations" refers to commercial organizations.

[9] Kip E. Jones, "References" (last revised 2002), http://www.solvency.com/bibliogr.htm (accessed January 2, 2007).

[10] Kip E. Jones, "Bankruptcy Prediction: Summary" (last revised 2002), http://www.solvency.com/bankpred.htm (accessed January 2, 2007). "While continuing research has been ongoing for almost thirty years, it is interesting to note that **no unified well-specified theory of how and why corporations fail has yet been developed.**"

[11] Adapted from The Chartered Secretaries Canada In Canada, Chapter 15 of draft course material. *Disinvestment, Business Failure and Capital Reconstruction* (2004).

[12] BBC News, "Buffet Warns on Investment 'Time Bomb,'" *BBC News*, March 4, 2003, http://news.bbc.co.uk/2/hi/business/2817995.stm (accessed July 2, 2006). BBC News reports Warren Buffet as saying, "Derivatives are financial weapons of mass destruction," and "The rapidly growing trade in derivatives poses a "mega-catastrophic risk" for the economy ... "

[13] James E. Sinclair, "A Review of the Derivatives Market," *Jim Sinclair's MineSet*, March 27, 2006, http://www.jsmineset.com/prnHome.asp? PrintPage =Y&OrgHTYPE=3&VAfg=1&RQ=EDL,1&AR_T=1&GID=&linkid=34 87&T_ARID=3555&sCID=&sPID=&cTID=-1&cCat=&PRID=- 1&cSubCat=&archive=&highstr=None+of+these+instruments+are+regulated&UArts=, (accessed July 22, 2006).

[14] The Chartered Secretaries Canada in Canada, Chapter 15 of draft course material, *Disinvestment, Business Failure and Capital Reconstruction* (2004).

Chapter 11

[15] Eleanor Laise, "Interview with Sir John Templeton", *SmartMoney.com*, April 1, 2004, http://chinese-school.netfirms.com/Sir-John-Templeton-interview. html, (accessed January 3, 2007), During the interview Sir John Templeton stated, "I've found my results for investment clients were far better here than when I had my office in 30 Rockefeller Plaza. When you're in Manhattan, it's much more difficult to go opposite to the crowd."

Afterword

[16] M. Ramsey King Securities, Inc., *The King Report*, no. 3513 (2006), www.thekingreport.com (accessed July 12, 2006).

[17] "Plunge Protection Team," *Wikipedia*, http://en.wikipedia.org/wiki/Plunge_Protection_Team (accessed July 12, 2006).

[18] "Executive Order 12631: Working Group on Financial Markets," March 18, 1988. http://www.reagan.utexas.edu/archives/speeches/1988/031888d.htm (accessed July 12, 2006).

[19] John Embry and Andrew Hepburn, "Move Over, Adam Smith: The Invisible Hand of Uncle Sam," August 2005, http://www.sprott.com/pdf/TheVisibleHand.pdf (accessed January 2, 2007).

[20] "M3 is back," *NowAndFutures.com*, not dated, http://www.nowandfutures.com/key_stats.html (accessed July 12, 2006).

Appendix A

[21] See Glossary.

[22] Nike, Inc., "2006 Annual Report," 2.

[23] Nike, Inc., "When Nike Breathed Its First Breath, It Inhaled the Spirit of Two Men, Phil Knight and Bill Bowerman," 2006, www.nike.com/nikebiz/nikebiz.jhtml?page=5 (accessed January 2, 2007).

[24] Nike, Inc., 2006 Annual Report, 2.

[25] Celia Wolf and Paul Harmon, *The State of Business Process Management* (Newton, MA: Business Process Trends, 2006), 14.

[26] William J. Murphy III, "One Weird Day," *LeMetropoleCafe*, May 31, 2006, http://www.lemetropolecafe.com/Pfv1.cfm?pfvID=5430&SearchParam=May%2031,%202006 (accessed May 31, 2006).

According to the *LeMetropoleCafe* website, *"The IMF has directed CB's not to disclose how gold is leased/swapped, only total reserves (proof below)."*

LeMetropoleCafe website continues with, "The IMF has denied this: "This is not correct: the IMF in fact recommends that swapped gold be excluded from reserve assets." Refer *http://www.gata.org/bofi.html (search "correct")."*

If this IMF statement is correct, it appears a number of countries and entities are not excluding swapped gold from reserve assets, in defiance of IMF recommendations.

It is arguable there have been accounting practices which could be viewed by some as deceptive and that from all appearances, such practices have been countenanced by the IMF. Again from the *LeMetropoleCafe* website:

"*Philippines: "Beginning January 2000, in compliance with the requirements of the IMF's* reserves ... , gold under the swap arrangement remains to be part of reserves and a liability is deemed incurred corresponding to the proceeds of the swap." Refer www.bsp.gov.ph/statistics/sefi/fx-int.htm.

The Central Banks of Portugal, Finland, and Italy confirmed in writing that swapped gold remains a reserve asset under pertinent IMF regulations. The staffs of the central banks of Canada, Ecuador, Finland, Holland, and Portugal have also confirmed this. Refer www.goldisfreedom.com/IMFgold.htm.

European Central Bank: "Following the recommendations set out in the IMF operational guidelines of ... developed in 1999, all reversible gold transactions, including gold swaps, are recorded as collateralised loans in balance of payments and international investment position statistics. This treatment implies that the gold account would remain unchanged on the balance sheet." http://solutions.synearth.net/2003/02/21

The German Bundesbank (the secret "swapper" of gold with U.S.) lists "Gold and Gold Receivables (loans)" as a one line item on its balance sheet. This deception conflicts with GAAP, and thus German banking law. So, from their published financial statements there is no way to determine how much gold Germany holds in its vaults."

Whether in defiance or in compliance with the IMF, a black hole exists if the following statement from the *LeMetropoleCafe* website is true, " ... has allowed official sector gold to hit the market without a corresponding drawdown on the balance sheets of central banks. This has made it impossible for analysts to ascertain the exact size of official sector gold loans, swaps, and deposits. The unwillingness of central banks to provide even a minimum level of transparency suggests that total gold receivables are substantially larger than the accepted industry figure of ~5,000 tonnes. Refer http://groups.yahoo.com/group/gata/message/903 ."

27 Sangita Shah, "Double Counting of Gold by Central Banks May Have Aided the Price Suppression," *Mumbai, India: The Financial Express,* June 6, 2006, http://www.financialexpress.com/print.php?content_id=129715 (accessed July 1, 2006).

28 David Shirreff, "Lessons from the Collapse of Hedge Fund, Long-Term Capital Management" (University of Washington, 1999), 3.

29 Bank for International Settlements, Monetary and Economic Department, "OTC derivatives market activity in the first half of 2006 (November 2006), Table 1: The global OTC derivatives market," http://www.bis.org/publ/otc_hy0611.pdf (accessed January 2, 2007).

30 Ibid.

Glossary

31 "Warren Buffet," *Wikipedia,* http://en.wikipedia.org/wiki/Warren_Buffet (accessed July 2, 2006).

32 *Dictionary of Current English,* 3rd ed. (New York: Oxford University Press, 2001), 167.

33 Corporate Streamlining Technology Inc., *Corporate Streamlining Technology Manual,* (Richmond Hill, Ontario, Canada: Corporate Streamlining Technology Inc., 2006), 50.

34 United States Bankruptcy Court, Southern District of New York, FORM B1 Voluntary Petition, Name of Debtor—Enron Corp., December 2, 2001.

978-0-595-42536-5
0-595-42536-4

Printed in the United States
75507LV00004B/166-501

9 780595 425365